BETWEEN THE LINES

GOD IS WRITING YOUR STORY

BOB SORGE

OASIS HOUSE
KANSAS CITY, MISSOURI

Editors: Katie Hebbert and Edie Mourey
Cover designer: Brian Griffith
Typesetter: Dale Jimmo

Printed in the United States of America
ISBN: 978-1-937725-07-5
Library of Congress Control Number: 2012949321

For information on all of Bob's books, see page 128.

www.oasishouse.com

To Andrés & Kelly Spyker

I dedicate this book to the delightful story God is crafting with your lives. Each of your parents went before you, making a way, and both of you said yes to the call of God. When our paths first crossed, you were dating each other. Now, you have two sons and an amazing sphere of influence in Mexico and the world. What God is doing with you has everything to do with your parents, and even more to do with your children. It's a living legacy for Mexico to read and follow (Heb. 13:7). We're eager to watch how God brings it full circle and finishes your story. May He give you a place in the great cloud of witnesses.

Contents

Part One: The Stuff of Story

SUSPENSE, INTRIGUE, ADVENTURE, ROMANCE

The Power of Story
CHAPTER 1

They sat spellbound in the darkness, hardly breathing. A few were occasionally nibbling popcorn while most just stared. The screen had transported them into a new reality. Left behind was the ho-hum, the mundane, the everyday; they were swept up into a world of excitement, adventure, intrigue, and romance.

They had entered the theater as individuals with impassive expressions. But now they were one, a group that swayed and played with the drama, faces open and eager. Anger, joy, love, hate, fear, excitement—a multitude of emotions were being shared together as the moviegoers became one with the screen. They laughed and cried as they went places never before traversed. Things were as they should be—wrongs were made right, evil was punished, justice was served, loyalty was rewarded, love was shared, the impossible was overcome.

They had come, not to escape from life but to experience it. Lifted above meaninglessness, they were now elevated into something higher, something for which their spirits yearned. Life was springing to new meaning in the safety of their seats.

Hollywood has captured the power of story. Audiences identify with the movie, locate themselves in the story, and connect with its significance.

Long before Hollywood, Jesus got the power of story. Case in point: Jesus healed a demon-possessed man, who then wanted to follow Him. Instead of allowing it, Jesus told him to stay home and tell his friends what God had done for him. (See Mark 5:1-20.)

Even though the people of the region initially rejected Jesus, He knew their hearts would change simply by the power of this man's story.

God has always used stories to convey His message to the world. Much of the Bible is narrative. Scripture has used the histories of biblical characters to inspire people for centuries. This is why God is also writing a story with your life. Like a masterful screenwriter, He is crafting your journey in such a way that when you recount it, others will be revitalized in their faith.

Sometimes life becomes so mundane that we lose perspective on our way. The story gets to feeling interminable. My main objective in writing this book, therefore, is to strengthen your grip on the divine purpose of your story. God has been with you all along—even in the dry seasons—crafting a fascinating history with the timeline of your life. He wants to see you through to the end.

VISA APPLICATION

Those who write stories have the ability, through the power of their art, to shape the values and convictions of nations and generations.

I was reminded of this truth while applying recently for a tourist visa. Invited to teach in a nation where Christians are often persecuted for their faith, I needed to apply for a visa in a manner that would not reveal the religious nature of my mission. In the process of completing the application, I came to the line where I was supposed to list my occupation. I knew instinctively that I should not indicate I am a gospel preacher. *Author*—that seemed innocuous enough to me. So that's what I wrote down, and sent the application off to an American agency that helps with my visa applications.

A couple days later, an agency rep called to say that if I put *author* on the application it would be declined automatically. That government, they informed us, does not want authors or lawyers visiting their nation.

I thought author was a neutral occupation and was initially surprised to discover they perceived it as dangerous. But upon reflection, it made sense. Stories are catalytic, and can pose a threat to repressive governments that do not want people to think for themselves or to form politically incorrect beliefs. Authors have the power, through story, to shape the ideals and principles of the land.

That exchange with the visa agency heightened my awareness of the power that resides in having a great story and sharing it with someone else.

STORIES GO DOWN EASY

One reason stories are so powerful is because they have a way of bypassing people's defenses and winning their hearts.

This is what happened when the New Testament church hit into what was perhaps the thorniest theological issue they would have to face. It was the problem of the Gentiles. How could Gentiles possibly be included in the church of Jesus Christ? The Jews had both an anti-Gentile theology and anti-Gentile sentiments. Anyone who even hinted at acceptance of Gentiles would be met with a blast of antagonism and hostility.

You can see the volatile emotions that boiled near the surface when this issue came up.

> *Now the apostles and brethren who were in Judea heard that the Gentiles had also received the word of God. And when Peter came up to Jerusalem, those of the circumcision contended with him, saying, "You went in to uncircumcised men and ate with them!" (Acts 11:1-3).*

Some of the Jewish believers in Jerusalem had problems doctrinally with the fact that Peter ate with uncircumcised Gentiles. They were convinced that uncircumcised Gentiles had no place in the covenant community of God. God knew that before the believing Jews would ever accept the Gentiles as equals in faith, they would need help to change their hardened positions on this super-heated issue. How could God help them make such a massive transition?

One option was to give Peter supernatural insight into the Scriptures on the topic, and then Peter could hold a teaching symposium in Jerusalem for all the Jews. If he led a comprehensive, three-week study, he might be able to get the main players on board, and from there the huge ship might begin to make a slow turn toward the Gentiles.

Instead, it's as though God said, "Let's make it easier for them. Let's help them. Let's give it to them in a story." By turning the whole thing into a story, God bypassed all the wrangling and theological objections that would have most certainly ensued.

So when Peter was accosted by the Jewish believers in Jerusalem about eating with uncircumcised men, he simply told his story.

> *But Peter explained it to them in order from the beginning, saying:*
> *"I was in the city of Joppa praying; and in a trance I saw a vision,*
> *an object descending like a great sheet, let down from heaven by four*
> *corners; and it came to me" (Acts 11:4-5).*

From there, he went on to tell how the voice from heaven told him not to call unclean anything that God had cleansed. Then the three men arrived, and Peter went with them to Caesarea. While preaching to the Gentiles there, the Holy Spirit suddenly fell on them and they all began to speak in tongues and magnify God.

Peter did not tell Cornelius's version of the narrative (which we have in Acts 10). In fact, he didn't even mention Cornelius's name. He simply told the account as he himself experienced it. He knew the story wouldn't convince anyone if he told Cornelius's version; it would hold power only as he told his own side of the story.

How did the Jewish believers respond? Amazingly swiftly. "When they heard these things they became silent; and they glorified God, saying, 'Then God has also granted to the Gentiles repentance to life'" (Acts 11:18).

Twenty minutes of story did more to win their hearts than three weeks of fiery debate would have.

Herein lies the power of story: It bypasses defenses and melts resistance. And this is why God will give *you* a story to tell. It can soften antagonistic skeptics and win them to the love and wisdom of God.

Stories also have the power to convince people in ways that straightforward, didactic teaching cannot always accomplish. We see this in the life of the apostle Paul.

PAUL'S DAMASCUS ROAD ENCOUNTER

Paul (named Saul at the time) made his way to Damascus to arrest those who believed in Christ and haul them back to Jerusalem.

There was nothing unusual about that day, he was just going about his business. As he approached the city, it's as though Jesus said, "Saul, get ready. I'm about to give you a good story."

Truly, Paul's Damascus road encounter had all the ingredients of an outstanding story. He was knocked to the ground, beheld the face of Christ, and had an audible conversation with Jesus Himself. The light was so bright that Paul was blinded and needed others to lead him by the hand. Those who were with him saw the light, but couldn't see the Lord nor distinguish His words. For three days and nights he neither ate nor drank. Then, as though scales fell from his eyes, his sight was miraculously restored. He was filled with the Holy Spirit, baptized in water, and commissioned as an apostolic herald to the Gentiles.

The whole story is *so* dramatic!

And when you follow Paul's ministry in the book of Acts, you find him telling this experience over and over again. Why? Because there's *power* on a good story.

Paul's Damascus road story had the kind of power on it that enabled those who could not grasp the message of the gospel to wrap their fingers around something in the kingdom and lay hold of their eternal destiny. Where gospel principles did not penetrate, the dazzling screenplay of a true episode could pierce the darkness and reach a needy heart.

God still does the same today. He writes stories with our lives that have such power on them that seekers can get a handle on the meaning of the gospel. A way is made for those who could not otherwise find their way.

What we need today, more than ever, are men and women with stories in God that are so compelling that they shift eternal destinies.

It's interesting to follow how Paul used his testimony. Whenever he found himself in front of a particularly tough crowd, he would pull out his Damascus road story. Why? Because it had power on it to defuse animosity and win the hearts of skeptics.

Jesus, write a Damascus-caliber story with my life.

King of Drama

CHAPTER 2

God writes with literary punch. His writing style will leave you with a Damascus-caliber story.

I've discovered something about God: He's got a flair for the dramatic. If it's a choice between black-and-white and color, He goes with the rainbow. God doesn't stay in the center lane; He flirts with precipices. His symphonies may start with soft-string serenity, but before they're done, the timpani are churning out a thunderous crescendo.

He's the King of drama.

JUST FOR THE DRAMA

There's some stuff God does simply for dramatic effect. Let me point to a few biblical examples, beginning with the exodus from Egypt. God could have extinguished Pharaoh in one moment and peacefully ushered His people out of Egypt. But that option didn't satisfy His penchant for pizzazz. It was too boring. God Himself said so explicitly to Pharaoh.

> *"Now if I had stretched out My hand and struck you and your people with pestilence, then you would have been cut off from the earth. But indeed for this purpose I have raised you up, that I may show My power in you, and that My name may be declared in all the earth"* (Ex. 9:15-16).

God was telling Pharaoh, "I'm not going to snuff you out with one lethal blow. I'm going to hit you again, and again, and again. With each hit the intensity will rise, until the whole thing reaches a feverish pitch of suspense. Then, when I deliver My people, My name will be glorified in all the earth."

What symphonic drama! Not just one, or two, or three—but *ten* devastating plagues exploded in Egypt, leaving the nation in shambles. Finally, Pharaoh let God's people go, only to change his mind and chase them into the sea. The whole ordeal is incomprehensibly dramatic. And what a fantastic climax to the plot! The Red Sea rushed down upon Pharaoh and his army and reduced them to bloated corpses on the beach.

There's no getting around it, God likes to make huge splashes that culminate in magnificent demonstrations of His mighty salvation. By the time it's done, people the world over have witnessed God's glory.

Look at another example: Peter in prison (Acts 12). He was incarcerated in Herod's prison for quite a few days, but look at when God finally decided to liberate him: The last night before his scheduled execution. God could have delivered him days earlier, but He waited till the last moment. Why? To crank up the suspense meter.

Why is He a last-minute God? Why does He stall to intervene until the tension becomes gargantuan? Why does He wait until "the break of dawn" (Ps. 46:5) to help His people?

Answer: He likes to make a name for Himself.

Would you like another example of God just being dramatic? Look at the time He delivered Paul and Silas from jail in Philippi (Acts 16). God watched while they were being beaten bloody and then placed in stocks. He watched while the hours ticked away, and Paul and Silas had nothing else to do but sing and pray. Then at midnight, KABOOM, an earthquake struck, all the doors of the jail flung wide, and the chains fell off all the prisoners. The jailer and his entire household got saved, and a church was birthed.

At first glance, it appears that God delivered Paul and Silas because He wanted them freed to continue their apostolic mission. But when you look at the story more closely, you realize that they were going to be released in the morning anyways. So why did God send the earthquake and release all the prisoners? Simply for the drama. They would have been released in the morning, but

God didn't want it coming down that quietly. He's into story. He loves to write dramas that shake cities, transform households, and glorify His great name.

God's ways are dramatic with both the godly *and* the ungodly. God takes the righteous through great difficulty in order to promote them in a dramatic way. But He does the opposite with the wicked. He builds them up on the front end so that the devastation of their latter end is all the more dramatic.

Haman is a colorful example. He was exalted to such a place of prominence in the kingdom that he alone was invited to a banquet with the king and queen—twice. That pinnacle of honor became the backdrop for the disgrace of his demise: He was hung the same evening on his own gallows. He went from hobnobbing to hanging in minutes. Thus, Haman was taken out just as Psalm 92:7 portended: "When the wicked spring up like grass, and when all the workers of iniquity flourish, it is that they may be destroyed forever." God purposely exalts the wicked so that the calamity of their fall will be all the greater.

In referring to the confrontation on Mount Carmel between Elijah and the prophets of Baal, Lou Engle has observed that God is always seeking to set up a showdown.

This is why Solomon wrote, "Blessed be the LORD God, the God of Israel, who only does wondrous things!" (Ps. 72:18). That's all God *ever* does—wondrous things. If it's not wondrous, He didn't do it. And if He did it, it will leave you marveling in gaping wonder.

There is nothing more dramatic, of course, in all of Scripture, than the scourging, crucifixion, death, burial, descent, resurrection, and ascension of Christ. Our salvation pivots on drama. The extremity and horror of the cross causes the glory of our salvation to excel in dazzling brilliance.

I love that we serve such a dramatic God! He may orchestrate the extremity of our humiliation, but it's so that the glory of our ultimate exaltation shines all the brighter.

Elements of Story

Riveting stories usually contain a protagonist (from a Greek word meaning, "one who plays the first part"), who is the main character in the story and who is in conflict with an antagonist(s).

The antagonist can be a sinister person, a towering challenge, a horrific ordeal, or even something within the protagonist himself that must be overcome. The story follows the protagonist as he or she pursues the quest for serenity and fulfillment.

Most protagonists in biblical stories are presented with either a seemingly insurmountable challenge that must be overcome, or with irretrievable losses from which no recovery seems possible. The lives of many biblical characters follow this general roadmap. Joseph's journey, for example, was launched by the trauma of being sold into slavery. David burst onto the scene by killing Goliath. Job was plunged into crisis through a bizarre series of same-day, devastating events. We know about Jonah because he was swallowed by a fish.

A Dramatic Launch

As in the above cases, the protagonist is often thrust into crisis mode through a catalytic event that suddenly changes everything, triggering an impassioned journey. Modern stories are often formed in the same way.

I relate to this personally, being launched into an unexpected journey in 1992 through a debilitating physical infirmity. Prior to that, I had no awareness that my life was an unfolding story. The injury changed everything. Since then, I am increasingly aware that I am living in a divinely-initiated story that is not yet finished.

Distress is not the only thing that can trigger a journey, but it seems to be a common means God uses. When life careens out of control, we go on a quest to find God's purpose in the thing.

The Bible utters a blessing upon those who find themselves on a journey: "Blessed is the man whose strength is in You, whose heart is set on pilgrimage" (Ps. 84:5). Oh, the kindness of God, to disrupt the safety of our comfort zones and divert us onto a path that becomes a divine storyline! The next verse says that the Psalm 84 pilgrim takes a "pass through the Valley of Baca." Baca means *weeping* or *tears*, so inherent in the metaphoric Valley of Baca is the imagery of suffering. How can one take a pilgrimage to Zion without it including the Valley of Weeping?

"They go from strength to strength; each one appears before God in Zion" (Ps. 84:7). No matter how or what may have triggered our pilgrimage, we are all headed for the same destination: God.

This thing ends with a face-to-face, eye-to-eye, heart-to-heart audience with the King. "Each one appears before God"—the boldness
of the assertion is a prophetic declaration over your life: You're going to make it! A thousand battering voices may assault your mind,
telling you that all is lost—but the word which lives forever declares
that you will have your day with the King. In your flesh you shall
see God! (See Job 19:26.)

This is why the psalmist went on to say, "For a day in Your
courts is better than a thousand" (Ps. 84:10). One hearing with the
King in His courts is better than a thousand days anywhere else
in His house. To say it a bit differently, one day of Glory is better
than a thousand days of Presence. I love the outer courts of His
Presence, but I'm not satisfied with the periphery. I want to wend
my way into the inner courts of the King—into the Glory realm—
that I might behold His beauty and hear His verdict on my case.

Job was a man God launched on a Psalm 84 pilgrimage. You
cannot make sense of Job's Valley of Baca until you see it in the
light of his bone-chilling, mind-squeezing, breath-taking encounter with God and His Glory. Job had cried out for just one day in
court with God (Job 23:3-4); then, when he got it, what did he
have to say? "I have heard of You by the hearing of the ear, but now
my eye sees You. Therefore I abhor myself, and repent in dust and
ashes" (Job 42:5-6). His vision of God changed *everything*.

A Psalm 84 pilgrimage culminates in an audience with the
King. An audience with the King, in turn, changes everything. A
face-to-face appointment with the King will bring dramatic closure to your current chapter, and usher you into the next.

Jesus the Consummate Author
CHAPTER 3

Jesus understands the power of story. That's why He told so many of them. Nobody has ever been better at it. He was a master at telling stories that both illustrated truth and promoted recall.

Most, if not all, of the stories Jesus told were crafted by Him. He not only *told* great stories, He *created* great stories. He was not just an exceptional *storyteller*, He was the ultimate *storywriter*.

Said another way, He's not just a *narrator*, He's an *author*.

The Bible calls Him an author (1 Cor. 14:33; Heb. 12:2). He's the author of our salvation (Heb. 5:9), which explains why it's such a great salvation. He wrote it! And His pen is crafting a vast story that we call human history (Rev. 5:1). With Jesus as the author, little wonder history is so captivating!

He's also the author of books. Actual, literal books. Take the Bible, for example. The Bible has made Him the best-selling author of all time.

But He's not limited to just books. He also crafts stories from the pilgrimages of men and women on earth. The careful quill of this consummate author fashions your life into a unique, riveting story. This is what Paul meant when he said, "you are an epistle of Christ" (2 Cor. 3:3). He meant that your life is a living letter, written by the hand of Christ through the agency of the Holy Spirit, and intended to be read by others.

People might view someone like me as an author, but I don't hold a candle to Jesus Christ—He writes stories with people's *lives*.

When you *live* a story, you obtain profound ownership of the journey. Every challenge you overcome leaves its own indelible imprint upon your heart. Then, when you talk about it, your entire being radiates the story.

You become the message. The word is made flesh.

When you *are* the message, you move people at the deepest levels. On the one hand, the lessons you have learned enlighten their minds. But a life message doesn't simply touch the mind, it moves the heart. That's because the journey has profoundly transformed who you are. When you tell your story, people don't simply experience a *message*, they experience *you*.

Scholars move the mind. They depend upon their research to sway the thinking of their hearers. Living epistles do more—they move the heart. This is why God takes you on a journey. He instills a message into the very fiber of your being so that you tell it with passionate ownership. God wants you speaking from your life, not just your library.

A Divine Script

It takes extraordinary penmanship to write a story with broken, flawed, self-determining souls. Shaping galaxies? Easy. Shaping people? Now, there's a God-sized challenge.

Nothing in the material universe—glorious as it is—rivals the glory God derives from fashioning the lives of human beings into a breath-taking story. In other words, He is more into you than the universe. His greatest aspirations involve bringing you to glory. Your story is on His front burner.

The universe is easy; you—you're the challenge.

When Jesus is the author, everything mundane and ordinary becomes part of a supernatural script. Today you may see only the mundane; but stay in the story and one day you will see the supernatural that was behind it all. God is still completing your story. It's not over.

The point of your story is to make God—not you—look good. If we come away impressed with your zeal and dedication and faith, we have been left with dry bones. But if we come away impressed with the grace and mercy of God, we have been brought to a tree of life.

The power of your story lies in the manner in which God intervened in your affairs. People want to know how God got involved in your journey. A series of natural events lived only at the human level carries little power to arrest. What grabs the heart is when we hear how God stepped into the regular-ness of everyday life, infused it with His power, and produced a testimony to His greatness. People long to be assured that we serve a God who interrupts human history and propels us into supernatural dimensions of holy adventure.

A host of men and women have gone before us who testify to just that—that God writes supernatural tales with ordinary lives.

A Great Many Witnesses

The Bible is filled with people whose lives demonstrate the power of story. These saints were described in Hebrews 12:1 as "a cloud of witnesses." Exactly who is in that cloud? The previous chapter (Heb. 11) mentioned some of them by name—great champions of our faith such as Abraham, Sarah, Jacob, Joseph, Moses, Gideon, Jephthah, Samuel, David, and others. The cloud is not limited, however, to just them. It comprises the overcoming saints from all ages.

> *Therefore we also, since we are surrounded by so great a cloud of witnesses, let us lay aside every weight, and the sin which so easily ensnares us, and let us run with endurance the race that is set before us, looking unto Jesus, the author and finisher of our faith (Heb. 12:1-2).*

I used to think that the witnesses in the cloud were looking down on us from the balconies of heaven and saying, "We're watching you!" But now I realize—they're not witnesses to *our* lives; they're witnesses to the grace of *Christ*.

They give living witness to the goodness and faithfulness of Jesus. The story of their lives testifies, "He is a good God! He is a faithful God! I went through fire, through rain, through flood, and through storm; I couldn't see my way, and at times feared for my sanity. But I clung to His hand, and held on to righteousness. And He brought me through! He led me to victory over my enemy, and completed the good work He had started in my life. His grace was more than enough."

Because they have proven God's faithfulness, the witnesses can now say to us, "Never give up. Never let go His promises. The

God who finished my story is unchanging—the same yesterday, today, and forever. He will fulfill every promise He has made to you. He will complete your story, too. He is good to His word. Trust Him!"

The verse describes them as, "so great a cloud of witnesses." The word "great" originates from a Greek word that indicates numeric quantity. It means that there are a whole lot of people in this cloud. Thousands—yes, millions—of saints throughout history have proven God's faithfulness, and now stand as witnesses to His trustworthiness. The cloud of witnesses is composed not of a tiny, elite group of spiritual super-heroes, but a "great" company of frail humans (like you and I) who made their way by God's grace into a powerful testimony. The inclusion of the word "great," therefore, carries this implication: Admission into the cloud of witnesses is *attainable*. It's available to all.

We want in that cloud! We want God to write a story with our lives that shows Him to be faithful and true.

This is why we lay aside those things that weigh down our ability to run and the sins that easily trip us mid-stride (See Heb. 12:1-2 quoted above.) We are racing for the goal of gaining our place in the cloud of witnesses.

Someone might object by saying, "My story isn't important. It's *Jesus'* story that is important!" You're right, Jesus is the all-important star of all time. However, His story is incomplete without yours. His is intrinsically bound up in yours, just as yours is in His. The Father glorifies His Son by giving you a story that points to the greatness and majesty of Christ Jesus. We want a story so that we might give glory to God.

AUTHOR OF FAITH

The writer of Hebrews went on to describe Jesus as, "the author and finisher of our faith." The word "our" in that phrase is not present in the original text; a more literal rendering, therefore, would be, "Jesus, the author and finisher of faith."

Jesus is the author of faith. This thing that we call faith is His brainchild. He masterminded it. Conceived it. Originated it. Designed its DNA. As the author of faith, He wrote its binary code. He knows how faith works because He created it.

Faith issues forth from Jesus. It always follows the normative pattern of Romans 11:36[1]—it is received *from* Christ, implemented and expressed *through* Christ, and culminates in returning *to* Christ in praise and honor.

So if you want to grow in faith, go to the one who made it. Faith is to be found only in Jesus Christ.[2] It must be received from heaven because it does not occur naturally here on earth. Either Jesus gives it to you or you don't have it.

As the author and finisher of faith, Jesus both initiates and completes your faith. He starts you off in faith and then leads you into its perfection.

He's the author of faith. And He's the author of the Bible, of salvation, of cosmic history, and of your story. Come—let's look to Jesus, the consummate author.

---

1   "For of Him and through Him and to Him are all things, to whom be glory forever. Amen" (Rom. 11:36).
2   "...with faith and love which are in Christ Jesus" (1 Tim. 1:14).

Alpha and Omega
CHAPTER 4

The book of Revelation contains the captivating account of Christ Jesus visiting the apostle John in a magnificent encounter. The very first words out of His mouth were intended to be attention-grabbing. "I am the Alpha and the Omega."

Jesus identified Himself four times to John as the Alpha and Omega—twice at the opening of the book and twice at the close (Rev. 1:8, 11; 21:6; 22:13). Of the other titles for Christ in the book, none get more prominence. The repetition was Jesus' way of underscoring His point. "John, take note! I am coming to you as the Alpha and the Omega."

What did Jesus mean to emphasize?

Well, He spoke to John in the Greek language. Alpha is the first letter of the Greek alphabet, and omega is the last letter. If Jesus had been speaking to John in English, He would have said, "I am the A and the Z." If He had been speaking in Korean, He would have said, "I am the Giyeok and the Hieut." If He had been speaking in Russian, He would have said, "I am the Ah and the Ya." In other words, "I am the first letter of your alphabet and the last letter of your alphabet." And thus by implication, "I am every letter in-between."

As the Alpha and Omega, Jesus was saying to John, "I am the very essence of the stuff that comprises *word*." In other words, "I am the living word." (See John 1:1.)

Furthermore, as Alpha and Omega, Jesus was saying, "I am the arrangement of words into *sentences*, because I am the truth." (See John 14:6.)

Additionally, as Alpha and Omega, Jesus was saying, "I am the stringing of sentences together into a *story*. Because I am the author." (See Hebrews 12:2.)

By identifying Himself as the Alpha and Omega, Jesus presented Himself to John as the author. He was about to use John's pen to compose one of the most controversial, dangerous, and compelling books of the entire Bible. Human history through Jesus' eyes—past, present, and future—is an astoundingly vast, cosmic *story*.

BOOKS IN REVELATION

With the emphasis on Jesus' identity as author, it is no surprise that Jesus wrote many books in this Apocalypse, beginning with the Apocalypse itself. Someone might argue that John was the author of Revelation, to which I would respond that John was more like the amanuensis or transcriber. But the Alpha and Omega was the one who conceived and wrote it.

Take a look at the other books in Revelation that Jesus authored.

Revelation 20:12 talks about "books" that were opened: "And the dead were judged according to their works, by the things which were written in the books." These books of judgment were authored by Christ. Someone might object to that assertion because the verse does not explicitly say Jesus penned them. But Jesus did say that He is the Alpha and the Omega.

Revelation 20:12 also speaks of "the Book of Life," which Jesus authored. True, the verse does not directly state that Jesus authored it. However, Jesus made such a strong point to John from the outset. "John! I am the Alpha and the Omega!" Furthermore, Revelation 3:5 says that if someone's name is blotted out of the Book of Life, Jesus is the one who blots it out. We conclude, therefore, that when your name is written in the Book of Life, Jesus is the one who writes it there; and when a name is blotted out, Jesus Himself blots it out. It is His Book (Rev. 13:8), and He is its author. Why? Because He is Alpha and Omega.

Another book is mentioned in Revelation, this time in Revelation 10. It says that John was given a "little book" by an angel, and he was instructed to eat it. John had to ingest the prophetic message he was called to proclaim. I believe Jesus was the author of that little book. On what basis? He is the Alpha and Omega.

When looking at all the books in Revelation that Jesus authored, you come to a "scroll" in chapter 5. It was sealed with seven seals. I am saying this sealed scroll was authored by Jesus. The Father must have conceived the content of the scroll, and perhaps the Holy Spirit sealed the scroll (because sealing is one of the things the Holy Spirit does well, Eph. 1:13), but Jesus was the one who wrote it. On what authority do I say that? On the authority of Christ's words themselves, "I am the Alpha and the Omega."

This scroll, written by Jesus, is really quite the scroll. Consider this: The living creatures of Revelation 4:6-11 are able to gaze continually and directly—without veil or sunglasses—on the immediate, manifest, iridescent glory of God; but they cannot look at this scroll (Rev. 5:3).

Jesus, what kind of stories do You write?

JOHN'S STORY

John's Apocalypse speaks of all the books just mentioned. But I see yet another book being written here by the Alpha and Omega, although the text does not call this one a book. I am thinking now of a living epistle. I have in view the story of the apostle John's life. The fact that he encountered Jesus as author had personal implications for John's story.

Jesus' visitation to John happened at a time when he was around ninety years of age. He was in exile in a Roman penal colony located on the island of Patmos. Roman prisons were not famous for their amenities. And John's ninety-year-old frame was probably feeling the aches and pains that naturally visit the elderly. Given his living conditions and his age, I can imagine John thinking to himself, "I'm ready to check out of this world. My race is just about over. I think it's time for me to graduate to glory. My story is finished. I've had my turn. It's time for another generation to take the baton and run with it."

Jesus stepped into John's world just when he was aged, afflicted, and thinking of heaven, and announced to him, "I am the Alpha and the Omega." With that declaration, Jesus was saying in so many words, "John, I am the author of your story. And it's not over. Buckle up, I'm about to write an entirely new chapter with your life." I speak of a new chapter in John's life because, up to this point, we have no record that Jesus had ever used John prophetically. Suddenly, at age ninety, John was commissioned to an entirely new vista of ministry. Jesus called him to trumpet a prophetic, end-time message that would reach every nation and generation.

"John! Not only am I about to write a *new* chapter with your life, I'm about to write the *best* chapter of your entire pilgrimage!" Jesus had saved the best for last.

You are never too old for Jesus to write a new chapter with your life.

NOT AUTOMATIC

Jesus is a magnificent author, but that doesn't mean the completion of your story is guaranteed. Just because you're a blood-bought, born-again, heaven-bound believer does not automatically mean that every chapter destined for your life will be written. Some believers will get to heaven with entire chapters missing from what God intended to write with their lives. Why? Because we are active participants in the unfolding story.

Paul indicated that he had to *fight* to reach the terminus of his race. "I have fought the good fight, I have finished the race, I have kept the faith" (2 Tim. 4:7). If we want all our chapters to be complete, we must engage in the race with great resolve.

Let me use the language of Philippians 3:12. "I press on, that I may lay hold of that for which Christ Jesus has also laid hold of me." Jesus has laid hold of you in order to write a great story with your life; however, for the story to be complete, you also must lay hold of it with tenacity. Earnestly covet every chapter God has ordained for your life.

Yes, you must contend. But be encouraged, you're not the only worker here. God is also at work in you! As you do your part, God does most of the work. "For it is God who works in you both to will and to do for His good pleasure" (Phil. 2:13). Rest assured, your story is in good hands.

I'M NOT THE AUTHOR OF MY STORY

There's a paradox here. On the one hand, I am fighting for every chapter God intends for me; on the other hand, I am resting fully in the mastery of Christ's penmanship. Although I am contending for my story, I myself am not writing it.

How do I know I'm not writing it? Because if I were, it would read dynamically differently!

David spoke of the Lord as, "The God of my salvation" (Ps. 25:5). He was saying, "God is in charge of my salvation. He is the one to decide how my salvation will look in the end, and how I will get there."

Most of us like to feel in control of our lives. We like to know what is coming next. We like to know how the journey will launch, how it will progress, and where we will land in the end. The temptation, when we feel out of control, is to take affairs into our own hands and attempt to oversee our own salvation.

Intrinsic to the life of faith, however, is being totally dependent upon God's providence and goodness. If we were in control, it would not require faith.

If I were writing my life story, it would look far different from how it looks right now. I would have never chosen this present path. To be honest, I have not always understood or enjoyed His authorship in the moment. But I always return to this: He is the author, not me. Once again I say, "Alpha and Omega, I surrender my life to Your pen. Write my story. You are a better author than I. I trust You. Write it Your way. By Your grace, I'm staying in the story."

Plot Development
CHAPTER 5

"Okay, I'm convinced," I can imagine someone thinking at this point. "My life is in the hands of the consummate author. I get that. But here's what I don't get: The plot. Why does God write such long stories?"

The plot represents the main body of our journey. It points to those seasons in which nothing seems to be happening. As God develops the plot, He also intensifies the suspense and intrigue. Most of our years are spent here. When the journey gets long, we often find ourselves grappling to understand where God is taking us.

Sometimes we may face years of silence from heaven, when it feels as though an answer is never going to come. We may go through years—and even decades—without perceiving any substantial divine activity in our lives. Someone might describe such a season as one's "wilderness years" (hailing back to the forty sand-swept years the Israelites sojourned in the wilderness).

For me, waiting on God at times has felt grindingly interminable. "Okay, God," I found myself thinking, "If You're writing a story with my life...*can we get on with it?* I mean, what are You trying to do here, anyways? Write a cliffhanger?"

His reply seemed kind and gentle. "I call fast boring." He is not interested in writing a story with your life that is some flash-in-the-pan, BOOM-BAM-ZIP thunder clap, and one minute later the whole thing is completely over.

He rarely writes short stories.

Jesus is a skilled author, and He knows how to write a good plot. He intends to inject some suspense into your story, mix it up with some intrigue and mystery, throw in a good dose of adventure, and cap it off with the spices of romance (because by the time the story is done you will emerge from the thing lovesick for Jesus Christ).

Someone might complain, "But why does God allow so many strange trials and bizarre twists along the way?" The answer is quite simple, really. He knows that you can't get a good story out of a boring plot.

Great trials make great chapters.

The trek might have you careening near the cliffs of Sheol, but in the end you will stand in the "cloud of witnesses," raise your hands to your beloved Savior, and through tears of joy lend the weight of your own testimony. "He was faithful to finish what He started in my life. I am living proof that His word is true. He only does wondrous things!"

MY PERSONAL JOURNEY

Allow me to talk about my own experience for a moment.

I was raised in a Christian home by godly parents, and some of the first words they ever coached me to speak were, "I love Jesus." My father was a pastor so I was raised in church. Most of the day on Sundays was spent in church—from Sunday School to morning service to evening service. When I was growing up, there was no such thing as a separate church service for the children. You stayed with the adults and just learned to sleep. I could sleep in church with the best of them. I responded to so many altar calls as a kid that I don't remember which time I actually got saved.

Once I was an adult, people would say to me, "Bob, please share your testimony with us." Instantly, my breathing would get shallow, and my pulse grow faster. I would begin to hem and haw. "Well," and I would pause to drag the thing out a bit, "I was raised in a good Christian home." (Pause for a moment, take a gulp of air.) "I've loved Jesus all my life." (Pause. Full stop.) That was it. I had nothing more to say.

I tired of that whole scene and found myself mildly grumbling, "Lord, my story is boring." It's as though He answered, "We can change that."

And wow, what a change! In 1992, the Lord suddenly and dramatically launched me on a personal journey with Him. The circumstance that catapulted me into crisis was an injury to my voice made worse by a bad surgery. Since that time, my voice has been very weak and painful to use. The injury forced me into a dramatic redirecting of life, ministry, and focus. I could no longer lead worship or sing, and eventually had to resign from pastoral ministry. Today, I am able to talk, but not much louder than a whisper, and every word is painful. When I speak at events, they turn the microphone to the edge of feedback, I hold the mic on my lips, and then I can be heard.

Initially, I was extremely despondent over the incapacitation. But then it began to dawn on me: God is writing a unique story with my life! He is my Healer (Ex. 15:26). It's not over. When the path is long and arduous, I remind myself that He's developing the plot. He's so dramatic—perhaps He's planning a bell-ringer!

I know Jesus is an exceptional author. He is going to finish what He has started in my life. But I also know what it's like to lose one's bearings in the wait. I identify with people who find themselves in the middle of a plot, look ahead at the path, and have no idea how it might lead.

In those times, I have gained encouragement from the wilderness years of the children of Israel as they came out of Egypt and headed for their promises. I would like to share a couple insights regarding the release from Egypt that have encouraged me greatly.

Never Assume God's Silence Means No

After the deliverance from Egypt, God reminded His people of what He had done for them. He said to them, "You called in trouble, and I delivered you" (Ps. 81:7).

At first look, that Scripture appears to be saying, "You called to Me in trouble and, BOOM, I delivered you." But it didn't come down exactly like that.

When did they begin to call out to God in their trouble? We don't know the exact time, but we do know that they were calling out to God in trouble when Moses was *born*, because the Egyptians were already killing Israel's babies at that time. They did not get delivered, however, until Moses was eighty.

When you do the math, you realize they were calling out to

God in trouble a *minimum* of eighty years before God delivered them.

Well, when you've been crying out to God in trouble for eighty or more years, and have received no answer from heaven, it's easy to assume that the answer must be no. "I guess God is saying no to us."

But let me ask you a question. Did God actually say no to you? Not likely.

Let me brag on God for a moment. He rarely says no. He is the God of the yes. "For all the promises of God in Him are Yes, and in Him Amen, to the glory of God through us" (2 Cor. 1:20). You can be assured of this: When God answers your prayer, you are almost certain to hear Him say yes.

And in those rare instances in which God says no—we learn this lesson from Hezekiah—you can still sometimes renegotiate.[1]

Never assume God's silence means no!

If God hasn't answered your prayer yet, here's what you should take that to mean: God hasn't answered your prayer yet.

And if He hasn't answered yet, don't conclude He's not going to. Believe in "the God who answers" (1 Ki. 18:24). Settle for nothing less than a mighty encounter with the God who answers prayer.

I am imagining a hypothetical conversation between God and one of the Israelites who had just waited for eighty years to be delivered. The guy is objecting with God over the length of the wait. "But God," I suppose the guy complaining, "You took *forever* to answer our prayer!"

And I imagine God replying, "But I delivered you, didn't I?"

"Well," the guy pauses. He wrinkles his nose. "Well...*technically*."

It's here that God gets a little upset. "What do you mean, 'technically'? Listen! If I've been writing a story for your nation to empower your people for *centuries*..."

---

1   I am referring here to the story in Isaiah 38 in which Hezekiah was sick and near death, and Isaiah went to him with this word: "Thus says the LORD: 'Set your house in order, for you shall die and not live'" (Isaiah 38:1). Desperate for God to change His mind, Hezekiah cried out to God with tears, begging Him for mercy. In response, the Lord healed Hezekiah and extended his life by fifteen years.

You have to admit, the deliverance from Egypt was *amazing!* Talk about having all the components of a good story—suspense, intrigue, suffering and consolation, exploitation and divine retribution, confrontation and victory—all the makings of an exceptional drama. The exodus from Egypt was such a powerful story that it has carried the nation of Israel for centuries—even to the present day.

"If I've been writing a story for your nation," I hear God saying to this impatient Israelite, "to empower your people for *centuries*, then give Me a little space to work."

God was giving Israel a story that would strengthen them for several thousand years. To give them *that* kind of story, He needed eighty-plus years to set the thing up.

Could it be that the duration of your wait is reflective of the significance of your deliverance? To say it another way, could the intensity of the plot point to the significance of the finale?

Give God room to work. And give Him something to work with. Those who assume God's silence means no tend to disengage, eject themselves from the plot, and abort the journey. While they walk away from the story, God's thinking, "If only you had waited on Me!"

If God hasn't said no, stay in the storyline. Wait on Him. Call on His name until He delivers you.

WHY THE CAPTIVITY?

While we're talking about the deliverance from Egypt, let me ask a question. Have you ever wondered why God placed the nation of Israel inside Egypt for 430 years? Here's the verse on it.

> *Now the sojourn of the children of Israel who lived in Egypt was four hundred and thirty years. And it came to pass at the end of the four hundred and thirty years—on that very same day—it came to pass that all the armies of the LORD went out from the land of Egypt (Ex. 12:40-41).*

Jacob and his little family—seventy in number—were living in Canaan (their promised land) when God sovereignly moved them to Egypt (Gen. 46:27). Then He kept them in Egypt a *really* long time, under *really* difficult circumstances.

Actually, many scholars concur that the 430 years mentioned here are to be measured from the time of Abraham. (See Galatians 3:17.) They calculate that the actual time the nation of Israel spent inside Egypt was roughly half of the 430 years, more like 200 to 225 years.[2]

Let's suppose they're right. Let's say Israel was inside Egypt for approximately 215 years. That's still a long time! And they were grueling years spent in slavery, forced labor, and harsh oppression.

What was God thinking? Why did He do that to Israel? Why did He take them from their promised land and place them in bondage for so many years?

I would like to answer that question.

In those days, the foremost decimator of human population was war. One reason was because some people groups had the practice of automatically going to war almost every year in the spring (2 Sam. 11:1; 1 Ki. 20:22). If God had left Jacob and his little family inside Canaan, over the years they would have been constantly attacked on all sides by warring tribes, raiding parties, territorial kings, and imperialistic invaders. Under that kind of continual bombardment, the nation of Israel would have been persistently cut back in size and would have never gained the critical mass necessary to take their promised land.

God's solution was to take them out of Canaan and place them inside Egypt. Jacob didn't know it, but God was basically saying, "Jacob, let Me do you a favor. I'm going to protect your family by placing them behind the front lines of the number one military machine on the planet—the army of Egypt."

During Israel's tenure in Goshen, she was protected by Egypt's army. For some 215 years, the nation of Israel did not suffer a single casualty to war. They just kept growing.

2   In Galatians 3:17, Paul seems to convey that the 430 years began with Abraham. John Gill (Online Bible) cites the computations of Pareus on the 430 years as follows: From the confirmation of the covenant, and Abraham taking Hagar for his wife, to the birth of Isaac, 15 years; from the birth of Isaac, to the birth of Jacob, 60 years (Gen. 25:26); from the birth of Jacob to his going down into Egypt, 130 years (Gen. 47:9); from his going down to Egypt, to his death, 17 years (Gen 47:28); from the death of Jacob to the death of Joseph in Egypt, 53 years (Gen 50:26); from the death of Joseph to the birth of Moses, 75 years; from the birth of Moses to the going out of the children of Israel from Egypt, 80 years, in all 430 years.

They grew so rapidly and profusely that, within approximately a 215-year period, Jacob's family of seventy grew to roughly the same population size as Egypt itself. When Israel finally emerged from Egypt, she was some three-million strong.

Now the nation of Israel was strong enough to *enter* their promised land, *take* their promised land, *inhabit* their promised land, and *hold* their promised land.

God's purpose in placing them in Egypt is given succinctly in Psalm 105:23-24.

> *Israel also came into Egypt, and Jacob dwelt in the land of Ham. He increased His people greatly, and made them stronger than their enemies.*

God placed Israel inside Egypt to increase them greatly. When the Lord said He made Israel stronger than her enemies, perhaps He meant that Israel actually exceeded Egypt in population size (exact populations are not known); or He may have been pointing to the victory Israel celebrated over Egypt and her military. Oh, the wisdom of God! For over two hundred years, Egypt kept taking all the military hits so that Israel could keep increasing. Israel multiplied on Egypt's tab.

God puts you into captivity to grow you.

Are you in a time of restriction, limitation, or constraint? *Get large.* Use the season of restriction to go deep in God. Your prison is actually an invitation to get large in intimacy, get large in understanding, get large in the knowledge of Christ, get large in righteousness, get large in holiness, get large in the word and prayer, get large in good works, get large in meekness and humility, get large in faith and hope, get large in servanthood, get large in love.

Never waste a good prison sentence. Turn your prison into an incubator. Is it possible to get so large that the prison can no longer hold you?

Don't let the duration of the plot and the intensity of the crucible disorient you. Jesus is still with you, skillfully crafting your story. If you will continue to abide in Him, He will so increase you in this season that you will emerge from the captivity large enough to *enter* your promises, *take* your promises, *inhabit* your promises, and *hold onto* your promises.

Power of Perspective
CHAPTER 6

"A re we almost there yet?" We've all heard that common question. It's a cry for perspective. When we're on a long journey, we want to get our bearings. How far along are we? How much further must we go? Where are we, anyways?

Similarly, in the journey of life, we constantly seek updated perspective as we move forward. Perspective involves looking back to survey where we've come from, and then looking ahead to see where we're going. Perspective can bolster the soul and strengthen the heart for the duration. It makes sense of the present. Without it, we are vulnerable to despair and despondency. We languish.

Perspective, in one sense, can be viewed as another word for faith. The natural eye looks upon the visible while the eye of faith sees the unseen (2 Cor. 4:18). Faith sees that our entire life is a grand story, and that today's challenges are just a chapter in a larger scheme. Faith gains God's perspective.

The Bible says we gain this kind of perspective by catching the updraft of eagle's wings and soaring in the Spirit to a bird's-eye vantage on our horizons.

> But those who wait on the LORD shall renew their strength; they shall mount up with wings like eagles, they shall run and not be weary, they shall walk and not faint (Isa. 40:31).

The only way we can see our journey through God's eyes is to be lifted above our myopic, earth-bound parochialism. Eagles' wings enable us to see circumstances from heaven's perspective.

We get there by waiting on the Lord.

This verse links waiting on the Lord with the swiftness of eagles. Eagles will soar into the heavens, then suddenly swoop upon their prey (snakes, rabbits, etc.). Waiting and swiftness...hmm. Strange bedfellows. Are they not polar opposites? But the Scripture says that waiting on the Lord produces a swiftness of spirit.

Eagles will sometimes perch and wait for the wind to awaken. Pumping their wings to the heights is too exhausting, so they wait for the wind. Once the winds commence, they spread their wings, capture the power of the currents, and soar almost effortlessly into the heights. This perspective enables them to survey a vast circumference and spot prey far below.

The verse says, "They shall mount up with wings like eagles." There's a promise in the word "shall." When we wait on the Lord— that is, when we gaze upon Him in loving adoration, listen intently for His directives, and refuse to move independently in our own understanding—the promise is that one day the winds of the Holy Spirit will blow. Once the winds blow, we can spread our wings of faith and soar to a place of divine perspective. Take note of the promise: If you will wait on the Lord, one day the winds will blow and you "shall" mount up to a heavenly perspective.

PERSPECTIVE ON THE CROSS

God has a way of granting perspective on pain that makes the journey purpose-driven. When you are suffering, God's perspective on your pain can make the difference between being a casualty or an overcomer. This was especially true for Jesus on the cross. Divine perspective enabled Him to overcome His cross.

God's perspective on the cross is seen marvelously in its first mention in the Bible. God spoke of Christ's sufferings all the way back in the book of Genesis. This is what God said about the cross when He looked at it from an eternal perspective.

> *"And I will put enmity between you and the woman, and between your seed and her Seed; He shall bruise your head, and you shall bruise His heel" (Gen. 3:15).*

In this verse, the Father was speaking to Satan about the cross. He told Satan that, through the cross, Jesus would bruise his head, and he would bruise Christ's heel. Looking at Christ's sufferings from a bird's-eye view, God described the cross as a bruising of Christ's heel.

On the day that Jesus was hanging on the cross, however, with nails in His hands and a nail through His feet, it didn't feel like a bruising of His heel. It felt like His entire being was being pulled apart, molecule by molecule. Because it was.

The same is true for you. When you are in the vortex of your trial, you feel like you are being ground to powder. You may feel swallowed up in pain. Overwhelming pain is, well, overwhelming. It clouds our ability to see anything except the pain.

When you are being crushed, you may lack perspective in that moment. But as you wait on the Lord and are lifted on eagles' wings, the time will come when you will see your trial through God's eyes. One day you will see that your trial was only a bruising of your heel.

Now, make no mistake. A crushed heel is *incredibly* painful! I do not mean to minimize the trauma of your suffering. God did not trivialize Christ's sufferings. By calling it a crushed heel, God was clearly acknowledging that the wound was real.

However, it was also a truthful recognition that the cross was going to wound Satan much more deeply than Jesus. The cross wounded Christ's heel severely, but it dealt a death blow to Satan's head. Jesus was *wounded* by the cross, but Satan was *destroyed* by it.

The cross was a bloody spectacle. There was blood on Jesus' head, on His face, on His neck, on His shoulders, on His arms, on His chest, on His back, on his legs, on His feet, on His cross, on the ground. Blood everywhere! But here's the perspective of heaven: *Satan was more bloodied by the cross than Jesus Christ!*

Jesus wants to give you the same perspective on your journey. Because you walked out the story in righteousness and holiness, eventually you will see that your adversary was much more wounded by your trial than you. One day you will look back on your cross and say, "Wow, that was intense! I really took in the heel. But my adversary has been bloodied in the head."

SEEING OUR AFFLICTION AS LIGHT

When we step into eternity and look back on our earthly afflictions, we will view them as "light" and "momentary."

*For our light affliction, which is but for a moment, is working for us a
far more exceeding and eternal weight of glory (2 Cor. 4:17).*

When we are finally standing in the glory of eternity, we will
realize that the degree of the glory in that age is disproportionate
to the severity of the sufferings we endured in this age. We will
wonder, "How could such a small amount of temporary suffering
produce such a huge amount of everlasting glory?"

We know we will view it that way once we're in eternity. The
thing is, we want this eternal perspective *now*, even while enduring
affliction. Paul wrote as though this perspective is available to us
now, in this life.

Notice that 2 Corinthians 4:17 does not berate the saint who
is overwhelmed by the trauma of his or her affliction; rather, it
provides hope to the suffering saint by granting illuminating perspective. Perspective is empowering—it will keep you in the story.

I want to emphasize here that the Bible does not rebuke the
suffering saint for feeling overwhelmed and grieved when in a fiery trial. For example, when the children of Israel were suffering
"anguish of spirit and cruel bondage" in Egypt (Ex. 6:9), the Bible
called it "cruel," not "light." It is biblical to be open and honest
about your pain. See, for example, the cries of Job, David, Naomi,
and Jeremiah in Scripture. However, Paul was given such stunning
perspective that he was able to say, "Guys, I've seen the bigger
picture, and this affliction really is light!"

Perspective enables you to look at that which is "cruel" and
"burdensome" and call it "light."

Ask God now, while in the middle of your storyline, to show
you how temporary and light your present sufferings actually are.
Wait on Him. Wait until the winds of the Holy Spirit blow. Then
catch the up-drafts of the Spirit and look at your trials from a higher plane.

DAVID'S PERSPECTIVE

One reason we all love David's psalms so much is because of
his raw honesty. He told it the way he felt it, and the Holy Spirit
endorsed that honesty by placing it in the Bible.

But David didn't remain under the burden of his trials. He waited on the Lord, and the Lord brought him to amazing perspective

on his trials. Here's what David said, in his latter years, about the grinding afflictions he endured: "Your gentleness has made me great" (Ps. 18:35).

David looked back on all the fiery afflictions God had brought into his life and called them gentleness. How could such intense trials, which produced gut-wrenching psalm-writing, be viewed at the end of the day as gentleness? Only by having perspective on where he started and then where he ended up.

David began his journey as a nobody, a nomadic shepherd with a heart darkened by sin. But he ended his journey as the most powerful king on earth with a glorious eternal inheritance. Comparing his start to his finish, he realized that the promotion was disproportionate to the pruning.

True, David experienced intense refining in his life. But in contrast to the glory, he realized that God's disciplines were actually mild. So he looked back on all his trials and called them "gentleness." What fascinating perspective!

Jesus now says the same thing about His cross. He now says to the Father, "Your gentleness has made Me great." Jesus, how could You call Your cross gentleness? His answer might be, "When I see the magnificent glory to which the Father has exalted Me and My bride, I realize that the cross was the gentlest way to get us here."

Now you can say the same thing about *your* cross. Eternal perspective enables you to view your cross as gentleness, empowering you to endure in your journey until you obtain the prize.

The centrality of endurance to the completion of our story is so pivotal that we will now take part two of this book to explore this theme. And since we have spoken of David, let's continue with his example.

Part Two: Staying in the Story

FAITH, ENDURANCE, DEPENDENCE, TRANSFORMATION

Schooled by Saul

CHAPTER 7

Waiting on God is an important element in virtually *every-one's* story. And it certainly was in David's. God taught him in this discipline by taking him through a special school—Saul's school.

At first glance, Saul looked like an antagonist, but he was actually a gift to David. From his front-row seat in Saul's court, David learned from the devastating consequences of Saul's blunders. Like many of us, David often learned best by watching how *not* to do things.

One of the greatest lessons David learned was by watching how Saul refused to wait on God. It was essential that David master this lesson so that he could cooperate with God's storyline for his throne.

The Bible records three critical times Saul did not wait on the Lord. The first one was when he was being invaded by the Philistines.

WHEN SAUL WAS BEING INVADED

Not long after Saul had been crowned king of Israel, the Philistines came to challenge his throne with a military invasion. They attacked Israel with an army that was "as the sand which is on the seashore in multitude" (1 Sam. 13:5). The armies of Israel were intimidated and terrified, causing the people to hide in caves, thickets, holes, and pits. Many of Israel's warriors fled to the far side of the Jordan to escape the battle. Those that remained with

Saul "followed him trembling" (1 Sam. 13:7).

Saul and Samuel had an agreed arrangement: Within seven days, Samuel would come to Gilgal, offer the burnt offering to the Lord, and then Saul and his army would proceed to the battle. After the agreement was made, however, God told Samuel to show up on day eight. God was going to test Saul by having Samuel get there too late.

As day seven approached, Saul continued to suffer attrition in his army. He was desperate for Samuel to come and perform the sacrifice because, as king, Saul was not authorized by God to make a priestly sacrifice. It had to be done by Samuel. But Samuel was late.

Finally, when Samuel did not show up by the agreed time, Saul felt he could wait no longer. The longer he delayed, the more warriors he lost. The situation demanded action. Desperate to galvanize his troops, Saul himself offered the burnt offering to the Lord.

No sooner had Saul finished presenting the burnt offering when Samuel arrived. Samuel had some very strong words for Saul's presumption.

> And Samuel said to Saul, "You have done foolishly. You have not kept the commandment of the LORD your God, which He commanded you. For now the LORD would have established your kingdom over Israel forever. But now your kingdom shall not continue. The LORD has sought for Himself a man after His own heart, and the LORD has commanded him to be commander over His people, because you have not kept what the LORD commanded you" (1 Sam. 13:13-14).

In essence, God was saying, "Saul, since you will not wait on Me, I will replace you with a king who will." Saul's refusal to wait cost him the throne.

So the first time Saul blew the waiting test was when the battle was going against him.

WHEN SAUL HAD BATTLE MOMENTUM

The second time that Saul did not wait on the Lord was in an opposite context. It was at a time when the battle was going in his favor. Here is the story in a nutshell.

God used Saul's son, Jonathan (together with his armorbearer), to overthrow a garrison of the Philistines. (A garrison was a Philistine military outpost inside Israel's borders. The Philistines used garrisons to enforce their occupation of Israel's territory.) Taking out the Philistine garrison was an act of war on Jonathan's part. God honored Jonathan's faith and entered into the conflict by sending help from heaven. The ground began to tremble and quake. God sent confusion among the armies of the Philistines, and they began to scatter in terror.

Meanwhile, Saul was back at the camp. He could see that the Philistines were fleeing in helter-skelter pandemonium, but he could not figure out why. A quick roll call revealed that Jonathan and his armorbearer were absent. Saul wanted to know what was happening, so he called for the priest to come with the ark of God. He wanted the priest to consult the Urim and Thummim, which was a divinely designed means for a king to receive communication directly from God.

The priest consulted God, but He did not answer. In the meantime, the noise of confusion in the Philistine camp kept growing. It was obvious to everyone that God was fighting for Israel, and yet Saul wanted to get God's perspective on what was happening. When the noise in the Philistine camp continued to increase, however, and still God did not answer, Saul said to the priest, "Withdraw your hand" (1 Sam. 14:19). Instead of waiting for a word from God, Saul charged into battle and led Israel to a mighty victory.

Saul did not wait for God because the battle was going in their favor and he was eager to capitalize on their battle momentum. He wanted to maximize the slaughter among the Philistines. Here is the fascinating part: Even though he did not wait for God to answer, the Lord still gave him a mighty victory that day.

God's silence was a test. "Will you wait on Me even when it means a weakening of your victory?"

Saul won the battle and failed the test.

When Saul Had Other Options

The third time he did not wait for God was most grim of all, sealing his fate. It happened during a great showdown with the armies of the Philistines.

The Philistines had gathered en masse against Israel, intent to take Israel out. The superiority of their strength was so intimidating that Saul trembled in fear. What to do? He did the only thing he knew to do—he inquired of the Lord.

Saul was so desperate for a word that he did everything he knew to get God to talk. He consulted with those who received divine dreams; he asked the priest to consult the Urim; he inquired of the prophets of Jehovah. But nothing worked. He used every means at his disposal to get an answer from God, but heaven was silent.

What should Saul have done in that situation? Answer: Wait on God. He should have said, "God, I'm not going anywhere until You answer me. Even if the Philistines kill us all, I'm not moving until I hear from You." I am persuaded that if he had waited on God, the story would have read very differently.

But what did Saul do? He made the greatest mistake of his life—he consulted a medium (1 Sam. 28:7). Since God wasn't talking to him, he went with the other option—a necromancer. He asked a medium to bring Samuel up from the dead so that he might receive military counsel from the deceased prophet. That move actually cost Saul his life.

God tested Saul repeatedly with His silence, and in these three major instances he failed the test. Watching Saul's repeated blunders, David developed a firm resolve in his soul. "When I become king, this much I'm going to do—I'm going to wait on God!"

Because he did, God was able to write an amazing story with his life.

May this same lesson be blazoned on your heart. May you have faith and grace to wait for God to write your story in His way and time.

David's Advice on Waiting
CHAPTER 8

As we follow David's story, we see a man who truly did wait on God. Let's look at some examples.

For roughly ten years, David had to run for his life from Saul. He must have been tempted, while hiding in the caves and forests of Israel, to abort the story. "I can't live like this," I imagine him thinking in a weak moment. "I'm going to move to some faraway land." But he didn't surrender to that. He stayed and waited on God. Not surprisingly, it was during those years of hiding that he produced some of his best songs about waiting on God.

There were two times, while on the run, that he had opportunity to kill Saul (1 Sam. 24:6; 26:11). His comrades coaxed him to do it, telling him God had set up the opportunity. But David refused to kill the Lord's anointed. He left it to God to determine Saul's fate (1 Sam. 26:10). Unwilling to seize the throne for himself, David was determined to wait until God openly gave it to him.

Even after he was king in Hebron over the tribe of Judah, he still had to wait another seven years before God gave him the entire kingdom. Ishbosheth, Saul's son, was king of the other tribes during those seven years, and David had the military muscle to squeeze him out. But he refused to do so, again demonstrating his commitment to wait on God for the kingdom.

Furthermore, after Ishbosheth died and the entire nation was given to David, he consulted with God before every war. He didn't dare any military excursions without divine instructions. This was

David's pattern—he waited to act until he had received divine wisdom and help. It was this commitment to God's voice that enabled God to write with David's life one of the most fascinating stories of all Scripture.

It's no accident, therefore, that David became the first writer of Scripture to trumpet the discipline of waiting on God. The patriarchs and Moses had modeled what it meant to wait on God, but David was the first to actually write about it. His writings laid the groundwork, and then Isaiah wrote the tour de force on waiting.

Because he waited, God fought for him time and again. The Lord's vindication was so stunning that David wrote, "Take it from a guy who has done it and proven the Lord's faithfulness in this area. It pays to wait on God!" (That's my paraphrase of Psalm 27:14.)[1]

COLLIDING WITH CONTROVERSY

Waiting on God is one of the most controversial things you can do. Everyone will agree it's important that you wait on God, but nobody will agree with how you actually go about doing it. Everybody agrees on the principle; nobody agrees on the implementation.

The first rule in waiting on God (they will teach you this in Waiting 101) is to shut up. Tell nobody. Because everyone has an opinion about how you are doing it wrong.

That is why David's statement in Psalm 62, which appears innocuous on the surface, is actually one of the boldest statements he ever made: "Truly my soul silently waits for God" (Ps. 62:1). He stood up in his generation and announced it to the whole earth: "Hey, everybody! Listen up! I'm waiting on God."

Bad move, David. Nothing brings out all the conflicting theologies of God's people faster than this business of waiting on God. Suddenly everyone disagrees with what you are doing, and they usually have a Bible verse to support their position.

You can't tell your father-in-law—he is waiting for you to grow up and take responsibility for your household. He will view your "waiting on God" as a smokescreen for laziness.

Others will despise your posture as a dead-end street. In their view, waiting is a total waste of time, an exercise in futility. They will tell you to step up to the plate and take charge of your life.

---

1   "Wait on the LORD; be of good courage, and He shall strengthen your heart; wait, I say, on the LORD!" (Ps. 27:14).

Others, who have their own idea of what it means to wait on God, will say you are using it as an excuse for your unbelief. If you truly had faith, they opine, you would access the power of God and step forward boldly into your story. No amount of waiting on God, they will say, is going to change anything as long as you are bound up in such unbelief.

When some people envision waiting on God, they imagine someone lounging by the pool and sipping lemonade. It's not a cover, however, for laziness or unbelief. It's actually the opposite. Waiting will demand every resource in your being. It's one of the most violent things you'll ever do. It will require focus, intensity, and tenacity. When you're waiting on God, you're aggressively putting pressure on the kingdom of God.

Here's how I define waiting on God: *Doing whatever it takes to stay in faith.* When you are waiting on God for the long haul, and God is intensifying the suspense element in your story, the greatest challenge is to stay in faith. Everything is screaming at you that this is accomplishing nothing. If you are to stay in faith in the wait, it will require kingdom violence: fasting, prayer, word immersion, and the violent pushing aside of every distraction.

David went on to say, "My soul, wait silently for God alone" (Ps. 62:5). Waiting on God is not what you do when you have exhausted all other options, your back is against the wall, and God is all you have left. It's what you do in the face of other options.

When David told himself to wait on God alone, he had so many options. As the premier king in the earth at the time, he had people lining up to serve him. Kings, allies, friends, professionals—everybody was handing him their business cards and saying things like, "Call me if you ever need anything. I'm yours, anytime." Everyone wanted to be the one who came to David's rescue. But David looked at all his options and said to himself, "No, I'm waiting for God alone. He is the one who promised it, and I believe He will fulfill it."

David was saying, "I know only one way to wait on God. And that is to wait on God alone."

In Defense of Waiting

The preponderance of the Christian life comes under the banner of "waiting on God." Most of our lives are characterized by long periods of perseverance, interspersed with occasional spurts of sudden divine activity. If waiting on God, then, is the lion's share of the Christian life, why does it get such a bad rap? Surely, in these last days, God wants to vindicate this glorious grace!

David expressed his zeal for this grace to be exonerated.

Let not those who wait for You, O Lord GOD of hosts, be ashamed because of me; let not those who seek You be confounded because of me, O God of Israel (Ps. 69:6).

Let me explain what David meant. He was devoted to waiting for God to finish his story. All his contemporaries knew that was his stance. His concern, however, was that others might look at his journey, see its unfinished status, and wrongfully conclude, "It doesn't pay to wait on God." David was zealous for the Lord's reputation. He was basically saying, "Lord, may it never be that someone would be discouraged from waiting on You because they viewed my journey as vain and futile."

In other words, He was crying for God to defend the discipline of waiting. "I'm depending on You, God, and now the rest is up to You. You must prove Yourself as the defender of those who trust in You. Start here, with me." David wanted others to see how he waited on God and then how God delivered him, so that they might be empowered to trust God for themselves.

I'm taking David's path. I'm going high-profile with my case. I want the whole world to know that I'm waiting on God. I want heaven to feel that pressure. I have set my soul in such a way that I will be ashamed if God does not answer me. And if I am ashamed, a generation that has watched my life will be confounded. God, is that how you want my story to end? Or will You rather rise in Your zeal and defend this grace of waiting by answering me?

I rest my entire story on the premise that it is important to God to vindicate those who wait on Him alone. The world calls this insanity, but I believe it is the highest wisdom.

"INSANITY IS"

There is a saying circulating widely in America: "Insanity is doing the same thing and expecting different results." The idea of the expression is that if what you are doing is not producing the desired effect, then change something. It is insane to think that you can keep doing what you have been doing all along and suddenly stumble upon a different outcome.

There is some wisdom in that pithy saying, and there are many areas of life where that principle is applicable. However, when it comes to the discipline of waiting on God, that idiom is not applicable. When waiting on God, you keep doing the same thing even though nothing appears to be changing.

That's why the world calls this insane. They think it's crazy to keep waiting on God when it has produced no immediate breakthrough.

Faith is idiotic to the world. Faith conducts itself in a manner that the world considers irresponsible, delusional, naïve, foolish, and pitiable.

But people of faith know something. We know that everything can change in a moment when God gets involved in the mix. Therefore, we will continue to stand firm, meditating in God's word, holding to promise, giving Him our love, and waiting for Him to speak. Call us insane if you want to, but we're not changing a thing. We're waiting on God!

No Stench

As I have waited on the Lord for my healing, I have received strong consolation from David's pen in Psalm 16.

> *Therefore my heart is glad, and my glory rejoices; my flesh also will rest in hope. For You will not leave my soul in Sheol, nor will You allow Your Holy One to see corruption (vv. 9-10).*

I was praying in this verse one day, and began to say, "Lord, I have been in this chapter so long now that I fear my testimony is beginning to rot and stink. Others are going to look at the duration of my wait and decide that God is not answering my prayer. Lord, is my testimony starting to reek of corruption and decay?"

An impression came quite strongly to my heart. "I will not allow it. I will never allow the testimony of my holy ones to become a stinking corpse."

This assurance carries me. I believe He will not allow His child who hopes in Him to see corruption. For me, that means that my stance of waiting on Him will not become a stench of death to others. He will turn it into an aroma of life.

SHAMED, BUT NOT ASHAMED

Let me close this chapter with one more comment on David's tremendous prayer in Psalm 69.

> *Let not those who wait for You, O Lord GOD of hosts, be ashamed because of me; let not those who seek You be confounded because of me, O God of Israel. Because for Your sake I have borne reproach; shame has covered my face (Ps. 69:6-7).*

David said that he was covered in shame; and yet he prayed that none be ashamed because of him. He knew *shame*, but was not yet *ashamed*. That's because there's a big difference between *shame* and *ashamed*. Let me explain.

Shame refers to the temporary feelings of reproach you experience when your story is unfinished. *Ashamed* has to do with how the story ends. To be *ashamed* is to finish the last chapter of your life without having seen God's deliverance.

When you're covered in shame, don't be derailed by that. You may endure shame while you're waiting on God, but at the end of the day you will not be ashamed. He will fulfill His promise, answer your prayer, and finish your story. Your last chapter has yet to be written.

David's counsel is unmistakable: Wait on God!

Isaiah's agreement thunders across the centuries, arresting us with its fierce authority.

> *"For they shall not be ashamed who wait for Me" (Isaiah 49:23).*

O the sheer force of the statement! It could not strike with greater impact. "If you will wait for Me, I will not allow you to be ashamed at the end of the day."

You may suffer shame while the story is being written, but He will not allow your life to end in shame. It will not happen. He will not allow it. You shall not be ashamed. You are waiting on Him and He will vindicate the witness of your life in the sight of heaven and earth.

Sudden Forward Movements

CHAPTER 9

God's writing style is unique. He'll take you through a long stretch in which there seems to be no forward movement, and then suddenly hit you with something epic. Just when the journey seems interminably boring, boom, God steps into the thing and catches you up into divine adventure.

Are things slow going right now? You've got to know this about God's style: Most of the journey is not bells and whistles; mostly it's methodical plodding. But when God interrupts your tedium, the flashes from His hand that catapult you into your next chapter are unforgettable—and worth the telling.

When we want to encourage someone who is in a long season of dryness, one of the most commonly quoted verses is Jeremiah 29:11, "For I know the thoughts that I think toward you, says the LORD, thoughts of peace and not of evil, to give you a future and a hope." What a powerful promise! When we see it in its context, however, it strikes us even more powerfully. The verse in its context reveals how God will move us into our next chapter by dramatically interrupting a long period of seeming inactivity.

The context of the verse was the Babylonian captivity—a seventy-year period during which God seemed unresponsive to the prayers of His people. Look at it from that perspective:

> For thus says the LORD: After seventy years are completed at
> Babylon, I will visit you and perform My good word toward you,
> and cause you to return to this place. For I know the thoughts that I
> think toward you, says the LORD, thoughts of peace and not of evil,

*to give you a future and a hope. Then you will call upon Me and go
and pray to Me, and I will listen to you (Jer. 29:10-12).*

Jeremiah cautioned them that they were in for a long waiting
period. God had a word of hope for His people, however. After
seventy long years of exile, God was planning a sudden and sur-
prising intervention, and the Jews would be allowed to return to
Jerusalem. The wait would be long, but it would end in a dynam-
ic and dramatic reversal of fortunes. God would restore them to
Jerusalem and His house of prayer.

God is thinking similar thoughts about your journey. He has
already prepared a plan for your deliverance. Even if you must wait
for it, He has planned a time when He will suddenly and dramatically bring you into your future hope.

The seventy-year Babylonian exile and the subsequent return
to Jerusalem is one of the most instructive stories in the entire
Bible about waiting on God. For starters, it teaches us about the
paradox[1] of waiting.

The Paradox of Waiting

A paradox is two truths that appear, on the surface, to contra-
dict each other.

The paradox of waiting is masterfully articulated in the book
of Habakkuk (a book that was written just a few years before the
Babylonian invasion of Jerusalem).

*Then the LORD answered me and said: "Write the vision and make it
plain on tablets, that he may run who reads it. For the vision is yet for
an appointed time; but at the end it will speak, and it will not lie. Though
it tarries, wait for it; because it will surely come, it will not tarry"
(Hab. 2:2-3).*

The paradox of waiting is found in these words: "Though it
tarries, wait for it; because...it will not tarry." Though it tarries, it
will not tarry. Huh? Does the promise of deliverance tarry, or does
it not tarry?

The deliverance does both. It tarries, and it does not tarry. Let
me explain.

1   The word "paradox" is not in the Bible, but it is a biblical concept. Proverbs
    1:6 uses the word "enigma."

Habakkuk predicted that Babylon was going to pillage and destroy Jerusalem and the temple. God promised His people through Habakkuk that the time would come when He would judge Babylon. This promised judgment was a "vision" that would empower Israel to endure the captivity. However, He would not judge Babylon right away. Babylon's judgment was going to tarry—that is, it was going to take a long time to arrive. They were to wait in patient faith for God to judge Babylon. As it turns out, they had to wait seventy years.

However, God added this assurance: "It will not tarry." What He meant was that once it was time for Babylon to be judged, it would happen swiftly. It would be a sudden fall, not a drawn-out military exercise.

At the time of this promise, everyone thought Babylon was invincible. The city of Babylon was so heavily fortified that no one thought she could ever be taken. But God said that not only was Babylon going to fall, she was going to fall suddenly and sensationally.

Sure enough, that is exactly how it happened. Just at a time when Babylon appeared to be impregnable, she was suddenly taken by the Medo-Persians—and the city of Babylon fell in one night. It happened so abruptly that the entire world was stunned.

So the paradoxical prophecy of Habakkuk was fulfilled. They had to tarry seventy years for Babylon's collapse to come, but once it came, it happened overnight. The Medes and the Persians attacked and took the city in one single night.

Here's the paradoxical principle about waiting on God: *Sometimes God takes forever to change everything suddenly.* He might take a long time to act on your behalf, but when He steps into action, brace yourself. God is on the move and the mountain in your way is going to come down swiftly.

This principle is demonstrated over and over in Scripture. Allow me to point to several examples:

- Noah waited for 100 years, and then suddenly the flood came.
- Job waited for the longest time, but then suddenly God broke in and changed everything.
- Abraham had to wait for 25 years to receive his promise,

but when it came, it came with an avalanche of divine activity and blessing.

- Jacob waited until he was 130 years old, but then suddenly the salvation of the Lord visited him.
- Joseph waited in prison for roughly 10 years, but when it was time for him to be released, he rose in one day from the prison to the palace.
- Moses waited for 40 interminable years in Midian, but then suddenly God released him to lead the nation of Israel.
- Naomi waited on God after the devastating loss of her husband and sons, but then God suddenly brought redemption into her life.
- David waited in exile for roughly 10 years, and then God gave him the kingdom.
- Hezekiah cried out to God and waited for His deliverance; when God finally sent His angel, 185,000 Assyrians were killed in one night.
- Anna waited on God in fasting and prayer for close to 60 years, and then suddenly held in her arms the answer to her intercessions.

God's ways with us are still the same. You may wait a long time for God to answer your prayer, but when God tips the domino, get ready. You are in for a ride. Your deliverance "will not tarry." And as my friend, Brian Ming, said, "He's worth waiting for."

One reason God delays your breakthrough is because He still wants to infuse more tension into your story. The stronger the suspense, the greater the impact of the story's climax. It's all about the praise of His name. He's crafting a deliverance for you that will direct maximum glory to the fame of His name. Glory to God!

Habakkuk gave us the paradox of waiting, but his is only one of many Old Testament books with a message springing from the Babylonian captivity. Another such book is Zechariah. In his book, Zechariah also brought out the truth that long periods of waiting on God are often interrupted by His sudden, powerful interventions.

WAIT FOR YOUR MOUNTAIN TO COME DOWN

Zechariah wrote at a time when the people of Israel had just returned to Jerusalem from the Babylonian captivity. The people had a massive project in front of them: rebuilding the temple. With such meager resources at their disposal, the prospect of building and finishing the temple in Jerusalem towered before them like an insurmountable mountain.

But God promised the leader, Zerubbabel, through the prophet Zechariah, that the mountain would be scaled and the temple completed.

> *So he answered and said to me: "This is the word of the LORD to Zerubbabel: 'Not by might nor by power, but by My Spirit,' says the LORD of hosts. 'Who are you, O great mountain? Before Zerubbabel you shall become a plain! And he shall bring forth the capstone with shouts of "Grace, grace to it!"'"* (Zech. 4:6-7).

In promising Zerubbabel that the temple would be completed, God placed before him a remarkable picture. He said it was like a mountain that would be leveled into a plain. If they would just keep enduring and keep building, God would fight for them and work a miracle. One day they would look up and see that the seemingly unconquerable mountain now stretched before them as a vast plain of possibilities.

Through Zechariah's prophecy, God spoke to the challenge Zerubbabel was facing and said, "Who are you, O great mountain?" God addressed Zerubbabel's mountain as a "who," not a "what." That is because the mountain before you will sometimes seem to take on a persona or identity all its own. It's as though you could assign a name to your mountain. (Fear, Depression, Cancer, Bankruptcy, etc.) Many mountains we face actually have demonic energy behind them to one degree or another. The question of "Who are you?" is actually directed against the spiritual forces of darkness that seek to hinder your journey in God.

"Who do you think you are, to stand in the way of My plans and purposes for My children?"

God called the mountain "great"—not because *He* was intimidated by it, but because *Zerubbabel* was. But God reproached the haughty pride of the mountain. "Who are you?", He asked. To God, the great challenge before His people was "less than nothing" (Isa. 40:17).

In this passage, the Lord contrasted between mountain and plain. The starkness of the imagery is often observed in nature. There are many cities in the United States that are built on a plain immediately adjacent to a mountain. Some examples are Denver, Albuquerque, Salt Lake City, El Paso, Tucson, Phoenix, and Colorado Springs. In each case, the city is built on a vast plain, and then when you come to the mountain, all the development stops and wilderness takes over.

It's on the plain that you have houses, schools, banks, restaurants, stores, industries, skyscrapers, traffic, agriculture, and millions of people. The plain represents that upon which you can grow, build, and develop.

It's on the mountain that you have rocky precipices, forests, wilderness, running rivers, wild beasts, birds of prey, and snow. The mountain represents loneliness, difficulty, adversity, resistance, oppression, and overwhelming challenge.

God declared that the looming mountain facing Zerubbabel was going to be leveled into a fruitful, productive plain that would feed and sustain multitudes. God wants to do the same thing with the mountain before you. As you wait on Him, the time will come when He will pull your mountain down and turn it into a plain of fruitfulness.

There is one mountain in particular that God turned into an especially fruitful plain—I am referring to Mount Golgotha. God took the gloomy, oppressive mountain of Calvary, leveled it, and made it into a plain that now feeds the entire planet on the goodness of God.

How do you turn a mountain like Golgotha into a fruitful plain? "'Not by might nor by power, but by My Spirit,' says the LORD of hosts." It is through the power of the Spirit that miserable mountains are made into fruitful plains.

God wants to take the very thing that tried to strangle every vestige of fruitfulness in your life and turn it into a level plain so that the stronghold of barrenness will become a garden of abundant harvest.

When Zerubbabel's mountain came down—that is, when the temple in Jerusalem was finally completed—Zerubbabel did not sit down and say to himself, "That fight is over. Now it's time to relax." The completion of the temple was not the end of the book;

it was the launching of an entirely new chapter. Said another way, the finish line was the beginning of an entirely new race. The work was now to begin in earnest.

The same is true for you. When your mountain is turned into a plain, it will not mean that your story is over. Rather, it will be the beginning of a brand new chapter. Now that a plain has been prepared before you, it's time to build a city on that plain. You will be busier than ever. It will be time to cultivate a harvest in many people's lives because of what God has done.

The cry, "Grace, grace to it!" is not spoken over the mountain. The cry of grace erupts *after* the mountain is leveled. "Grace, grace" is spoken to the *plain*. Why? Because now that the mountain has been made into a plain, there is an entire plain that needs to be cultivated and developed. If ever you needed grace, it will be now! Masses will be drawn to the newly leveled plain and it will be time to build a city.

Zechariah's message is very similar to Habakkuk's. After a long season of waiting and enduring, God will suddenly turn an impossible mountain into a fruitful plain. The long wait will be followed by sudden divine activity.

Get ready for the same. The transition from this chapter to the next is likely to be swift and dramatic.

We have looked at Zerubbabel's mountain; now let's consider Caleb's mountain.

CALEB'S STORY

When you are telling some of the greatest stories God has written with people's lives in the Bible, you have to include Caleb. The story of his life is simply fantastic.

Caleb is the guy in the Bible who got a raw deal. He is the guy who had faith to go into the promised land, but because the other guys did not have faith to go in, he had to do forty years in the wilderness with a host of grousing unbelievers.

That is a raw deal. I said, "God, that's mean."

It's as though God replied, "Look one more time at Caleb's story."

After Caleb had done the forty years in the wilderness, had entered Canaan, and the land had been subdued, it was time for the land to be allocated to the Israelites. Joshua was the one who divvied up the land by inheritance to everyone.

Joshua said to each one as they came, "You get a house in a field." (The wars of Canaan had left plenty of vacant houses waiting for a tenant.)

"And you get a house in a field."

To another, "You get a house in a field."

To yet another, "You get a house on a wall." (It was customary in those days to build houses right into the walls that surrounded cities.)

All day long, Joshua would assign portions. "You get a house in a field." "You get a house on a wall."

And then it was Caleb's turn.

Caleb was like, "I don't just want a house in a field. I want a mountain." I can imagine some shrew scowling, "Who does Caleb think he is, asking for a mountain? Everyone else is only getting a house in a field."

But in actuality, I do not think anybody complained. Their response was probably more like, "Caleb wants a mountain? Give him a mountain!"

Why were they so willing for Caleb to inherit an entire mountain? Because Caleb had done the time. He had persevered in the wilderness for forty years. He spent enough time in the wilderness that he gained the authority with God and the credibility with man to ask for—and to take—an entire mountain in the grace of God.

There was a time when Caleb would have been happy with a house in a field. But after you have endured for forty years in a wilderness, you no longer want what you once wanted. *The wilderness has a way of changing what you ask for.* Prior to the wilderness, Caleb would have asked for a house in a field; but after the wilderness, he wanted more. Now, he wanted a mountain.

I can imagine God, before the wilderness years, thinking to Himself, "Caleb, I love you. You are My kind of man. I love your faith and devotion. I have great things for you. I want to give you an entire mountain in grace. But if I give you a mountain now, on this side of the wilderness, the outcry from the nation will be loud and indignant. Everyone will consider it unjust if I give you your mountain now. So here is what we will do. I will take you through forty years in a flea-enhanced, lice-infested, scorpion-enriched, serpent-strewn wilderness. If you will endure in faith through this vast dust-bowl, by the time you come out the other side, you will have gained the authority with the people to ask for an entire mountain."

There are some realms of authority in the kingdom that can be gained only by doing the time. You must traverse the vastness of the wilderness. If you endure, you will emerge with the authority to take and inhabit great mountains for the kingdom of God.

Do the time. Endure the plot. Let God write the story. Today, more than ever, we need spiritual mothers and fathers who have persevered through the wilderness and have bought the authority with God and the credibility with man to ask for and to take an entire mountain in the grace of God.

Before we close this chapter, look with me at just one more wilderness verse.

GOD SHAKES THE WILDERNESS

This is possibly my favorite wilderness verse in the Bible:

The voice of the LORD shakes the wilderness; the LORD shakes the Wilderness of Kadesh (Ps. 29:8).

It was an eleven-day trek on foot to get from Mount Sinai (where God gave the Law) to Kadesh[2], which was on the outskirts of Canaan. Kadesh was the place in the wilderness from which Moses sent the twelve spies into Canaan. They came back to Kadesh with a good report about the fruit of the land, but a bad report about the possibilities of conquering the giants in the land. Because of their unbelief, the nation of Israel wandered circuitously in the wilderness for almost forty years.

After thirty-eight years of wilderness wanderings, they returned to Kadesh a second time. It was during this second stay in Kadesh that God informed them their wanderings were over. He was now going to take them on a purposeful path into the land of Canaan.

Kadesh represents the place in your journey where you recognize that, after years of wandering, you have come full circle and

2 "It is eleven days' journey from Horeb by way of Mount Seir to Kadesh Barnea" (Deut. 1:2).

are back where you started. And now God shakes your wilderness and declares with His mighty voice, "It's time to go in. I am now taking you into your promises."

Kadesh is that place where God interrupts your aimlessness, breaks you free of the rut by the power of His voice, and launches you on a new trajectory into your promised land. After years of waiting on God, you are suddenly thrust forward into your destiny.

Perhaps your wilderness feels interminably long and pointless, but keep on walking and following the Holy Spirit. One day the voice of the Lord will shake your Wilderness of Kadesh and set you on a new course of purpose and promise. Persevere until His voice catapults you into your next chapter.

Toughest Verse in the Bible
CHAPTER 10

When you're waiting for God to bring closure to a long wilderness season, there's a Scripture that is the most challenging verse in the Bible to master.

Actually, the idea contained in this verse is also present in other passages. It appears compellingly in Habakkuk 3:16-19, and has hints in some other passages. But it occurs most succinctly and straightforwardly in the book of James. Here it is.

My brethren, count it all joy when you fall into various trials (James 1:2).

Toughest verse in the Bible.

Somebody might counter, "I don't think that verse is so hard. I don't think it's so difficult to be joyful in trials." You might feel that way—until a big enough trial comes along. Let something like Job's trial hit your life, and you will be overwhelmed at how challenging this little verse is.

James refers to "various trials." Trials is just a polite word for pain.

"Count it all joy when your pain thresholds explode through the roof."

"Count it all joy when you get blindsided by cancer."

"Count it all joy when your spouse divorces you."

"Count it all joy when your child has a car accident and is hanging on for life in the ICU."

"Count it all joy when you lose your job."

"Count it all joy when your house goes into foreclosure."

"Count it all joy when your daughter gets pregnant out of wedlock."

"Count it all joy when you have a heart attack."

If the verse had said, "Count it all depression," you could have done that easily enough. Because when you fall into a grievous trial, depression is often one of your first responses. Despondency is connected to the absence of joy. So the verse is saying, "Don't go in the direction of your first intuitive response. Everything inside you wants to be depressed right now, but the word of the Lord to you is, get into joy. Become joyful in the agony."

How do we count it all joy in the midst of horrific circumstances? The path is found in the next two verses.

> *Knowing that the testing of your faith produces patience. But let patience have its perfect work, that you may be perfect and complete, lacking nothing (James 1:3-4).*

"Patience" is not the best word to translate the Greek word in the original text. "Endurance" (or "perseverance") is more accurate. "Knowing that the testing of your faith produces endurance." Let me define endurance in the language of that verse.

DEFINING ENDURANCE

Endurance is *faith sustained long-term in the midst of trials.*

When all hell busts loose in your life, and you resolve to do whatever it takes to stay in faith, *that* is biblical endurance. Endurance is the resolve to hold to faith, in the midst of pain, no matter how difficult circumstances become.

To stay in faith while experiencing trauma demands the wholehearted devotion of spiritual violence (Mat. 11:12). Fasting, prayer, and word immersion are the key components in this violent resolve. Desolation has laid waste, and faith in God's purposes and intervention must be gained.

When you stay in faith in the midst of a painful trial, you are releasing the most powerful forces imaginable in the kingdom of God. Endurance (faith that sustains through pain) is so life-changing that it has the ability to do in you what nothing else can do. This is what verse 4 is pointing to: "But let endurance have its perfect work, that you may be perfect and complete, lacking nothing."

When you endure in faith, you release forces that have the power to transform everything about you. It is possible to be so transformed that you emerge from the trial "perfect and complete, lacking nothing."

That is the fattest promise of the Bible. There are other Bible promises that equal it (such as Ephesians 3:19), but I dare you to find a stronger promise than James 1:4. "Perfect and complete, lacking nothing."

The toughest verse in the Bible is likely to trip you up unless you see its juxtaposition to the fattest promise in the Bible.

What does it look like, to be made perfect and complete, lacking nothing?

Lacking nothing in grace; lacking nothing in the knowledge of Christ; lacking nothing in intimacy with God; lacking nothing in righteousness; lacking nothing in holiness; lacking nothing in love, joy, peace, patience, goodness, kindness, faithfulness, gentleness, self-control; lacking nothing in the gifts of the Spirit; laying hands on the sick and they recover; lacking nothing in spiritual authority; lacking nothing in meekness; lacking nothing in wisdom; lacking nothing in power; lacking nothing in faith; casting out demons; lacking nothing in good works; lacking nothing in giving; subjugating the works of the flesh; not loving your life even unto death; lacking nothing in discernment.

Perfect in doctrine; perfect in prayer; perfect in hope; perfect in servanthood; perfect in humility; perfect in speech; perfect in consecration; perfect in the fear of the Lord; perfect in the will of God; filled with all the fullness of God.

"Perfect and complete, lacking nothing." The implications of that promise are stunning. Endurance is the most powerful agent for personal transformation in the entire kingdom!

If there is a path to perfection that circumvents the suffering of trials, I do not know it. I do know that there is a time-proven, God-ordained, Bible-endorsed, sure-fire pathway to perfection. So if God puts you in a trial, maximize the opportunity. Wring from the thing every ounce of gold you can possibly buy.[1]

When your spirit is gripped with the realization that God is using your trial to perfect you in a way that nothing else could,

1   "I counsel you to buy from Me gold refined in the fire, that you may be rich" (Rev. 3:18).

guess what starts to touch your soul. Joy! What hell sought to curse you with, heaven designed to use for your greatest blessing. You are on a path with God that is headed inexorably toward answered prayer.

PROMISE OF INTERVENTION

At the time of this writing, I've been enduring in a trial for twenty years. I've become aware in this unfolding story that God has been changing me more deeply and profoundly than ever before. I feel like I'm in God's accelerated course.

So I decided to step back and graph my progress over these twenty years. Looking at my trajectory of accelerated growth, I reckoned that if He continues to change me at this current rate, I will attain unto "perfect and complete, lacking nothing" in approximately 436 years.

And I got depressed all over again! "I'm *never* going to get there!"

That's when it hit me. There's a great promise hidden inside James 1:4. It's the promise that if I will remain in faith over the long haul, even though distressed by my trial, there's coming a day when He will interrupt my trajectory and do for me what I cannot do for myself. He'll intervene and move me toward the prize in a supernatural way.

In other words, when I endure in faith long-term, I am on a collision course with a divine encounter of biblical proportions. He will meet me in His lovingkindness and carry me to the completion of my present chapter.

With long life I will satisfy him, and show him My salvation (Ps. 91:16).

For *this* kind of hope I can count it all joy!

Abraham's Unwavering Faith
CHAPTER 11

When I'm looking for a biblical example of how God brings closure to a seemingly interminable wait, I like to look at Abraham. He's the guy who had that arduous, twenty-five-year chapter.

When Abraham was seventy-five years old, God gave him a promise of a miracle baby, assuring him that he would be a father of many nations (Gen. 12:1-4). However, Abraham did not receive his miraculous son until he was one hundred years old. For twenty-five years, nothing happened. No miracle, no baby, no breakthrough. Abraham endured uncertainty and inner conflict, waiting for God to fulfill His promise. God was using the inactivity to ratchet up the suspense element in his story.

It's that twenty-five-year period of seeming inactivity that is referenced by Paul in this verse:

> *He did not waver at the promise of God through unbelief, but was strengthened in faith, giving glory to God (Rom. 4:20).*

When the verse describes Abraham "giving glory to God," it is pointing to Abraham's practice of declaring God's promise with his mouth. Abraham would tell people, "God has given me a promise, and He is going to fulfill His word." Even when he had no indication that God was doing anything, he still gave glory to God by affirming that God would be good to His word.

Abraham's example teaches us that we don't have to wait to receive our breakthrough before we give glory to God. We can give Him glory even while He's in the process of writing the story.

Pride wants us to shut up. Pride says, "Don't tell people God is going to answer your prayer. What if He doesn't? Then you'll *really* look foolish. Go low. Be humble. Keep quiet, until God answers."

But keeping your mouth shut is false humility. It's just a carnal way to preserve pride. To exercise true humility, open your mouth and declare what God is going to do for you. Give Him glory!

HE DID NOT WAVER

The verse declares that Abraham "did not waver at the promise of God through unbelief." *But God, how can You say that? Have You ever read the Bible?*

Anybody who has read Genesis knows that statement is not true. If you've read Abraham's story, you know that if ever anybody wavered in unbelief, it was Abraham. He was an up-and-down, wishy-washy roller coaster. He took wavering to a whole new level. He mastered the art of wavering.

What do You mean, God, by saying, "He did not waver?"

Perhaps you've read the story about the time Abraham and Sarah put their heads together to help God supply their promise. God was not coming through with their baby, and they didn't know what He was thinking. Were they demanding too much of Him? Did He need help out of a jam? Whatever their thinking, they decided to enlist the help of a surrogate mother—and ended up with Ishmael (Gen. 16:1-16). *Hello, God, we have the baby to prove it. What do You mean, he did not waver?*

Perhaps you've read the story (Gen. 20:1-18) when Abraham said to his wife, "Sweetheart, please tell the king that you're my sister." You see, Sarah was a good-looker. So Abraham pled with her, "Honey, if the king knows that you're my wife, he will kill me to have you. So please do me a favor. Save my life. Tell the man you're my sister."

If I were to try that trick with my wife, she would definitely think that I was wavering. And Abraham pulled that stunt *twice.*

"He did not waver" (Rom. 4:20). *You've got to be kidding! Come on, God, get serious.* If anybody wavered it was Abraham. The guy was an examplar of wavering. Not only did he waver—he wavered right up to the end.

STRENGTHENED IN FAITH

Even so, the Holy Spirit testifies, "He did not waver at the promise of God through unbelief, but was strengthened in faith." The Holy Spirit testifies that from the time Abraham received the promise until he received the fulfillment, he was "strengthened in faith."

Let me chart the verse for you, so you can see in graph form what the verse is saying. In the diagram below, the rising arrow represents Abraham's growing faith.

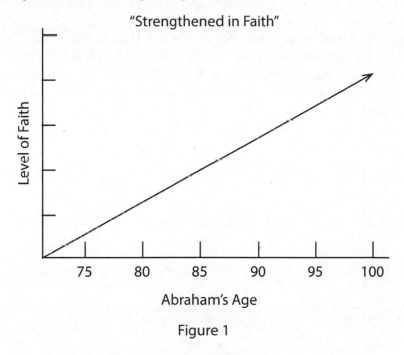

Figure 1

The Holy Spirit declares that from the time Abraham was seventy-five until he was one hundred, he was "strengthened in faith."

To say it another way, *the longer Abraham's answer was delayed, the stronger his faith got.*

Did you get that? Let me say it again. The longer Abraham went without his answer, the stronger he became in faith. Let me say it again. The longer he was without his miracle, the more he believed God for it.

That's irrational. That doesn't make sense to the natural mind.

Any rational thinker knows it doesn't work like that. Common sense says that the longer we're without something, the less our chances of getting it. The rational mind is like, "After all these years, it's time to square up with the facts. Wake up and smell the coffee. You've been waiting how long now for your answer from God? Five years? Ten years? Fifteen years? Time to get in reality. You ain't got it, fella, because you ain't gonna get it."

That's the voice of reason. That voice makes sense. We understand that kind of logic.

So what kind of faith is this, that gets stronger the longer it is without God's answer?

It's kingdom faith. It's Abraham faith. It's God faith.

I'm going to tweak our graph to more accurately represent what's going on in this verse. In the chart below, I want you to see how Abraham had his moments of wavering even while he was being strengthened in faith.

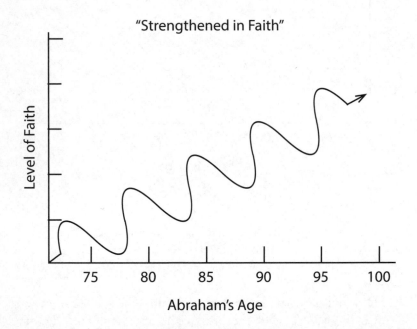

Abraham was a wishy-washy roller coaster the whole way, but when you look at where he started, and compare it with where he ended, it's clear that he was strengthened in faith.

God was not looking at the ups and downs of Abraham's emotions and feelings; God was looking at his faith trajectory.

Yes, Abraham had low times. He had times when his faith would crumble and deflate. But for every valley in Abraham's timeline, he found a way to pull out of the funk and rise again in true faith. When he hit a low place, Abraham developed a mechanism in God whereby he would encourage himself in the Lord. He would wrap his fingers around God's promise all over again, and affirm with all his heart, "No, I will not surrender to the voices of unbelief. God spoke to me. I know it was God. I know it was His voice. He gave me that word. And I know that God is true to His word. He is going to fulfill His promise. He is going to finish my story. It's not over. I believe God!"

Rising in true confidence, faith would again fill Abraham's sails. Every dip was followed with a subsequent rise.

God looked at Abraham's trajectory over the years, saw that he had more faith than he had years earlier, and declared over his life, "He did not waver."

GOD'S MATH

Here's how God does the math. He looks at all the dips in your journey and takes off all your lows—because He's not depressed when you are. Then He looks at all the peaks in your journey and takes off all your highs—because when you're having a "prophetic moment," He's really not that impressed. Once He evens out all your lows and highs, you're left with your trajectory (and we're back to Figure 1). When God sees that your trajectory is rising, He declares over your life, "He did not waver."

God doesn't measure your spiritual journey in *days*. Somebody might say, "Ouch, that was a tough day!" But God pays it no attention. He doesn't even notice when you have a bad day.

God doesn't even measure your spiritual journey in *weeks*. Someone sighs, "Last week? Ugh! What a horrible week!" God doesn't give it a second thought.

God doesn't even measure your spiritual journey in *months*. You might think to yourself, "Thank God last month is over! Whew, the month from hell!" It doesn't even appear as a blip on God's screen.

The issue with God is not whether you had a good day or bad

day; a good week or bad week; a good month or bad month. The question with God is this: *Where will you be this time next year?*

Get this. *God measures your journey in years.*

God's not asking whether you're having a good week or month. The question with God is, are you on a trajectory with Him in which you will be strengthened in faith a year from now?

God's question is, where will you be in five years? Where will you be in ten years? Where will you be in twenty years? Will you be growing in faith, giving glory to God?

This truth is liberating for me personally because I am a roller coaster extraordinaire. Sometimes I feel like a professional waverer. I'm one thing at 9:00 a.m. and something different at 2:00 p.m. And I don't pay it any attention anymore.

In fact, don't even ask me what kind of day I'm having, because I couldn't care less. Good day/bad day; good week/bad week; good month/bad month—makes no difference. Why? Because I've got my sights on next year. On ten years. On twenty years.

By the grace of God, I'm going to keep pressing into His word and Spirit, and by this time next year I will be stronger in faith than I am today. Why? Because I'm being "strengthened in faith!"

REFUSING ACCUSATION

Somebody might say to me, "Bob, the reason you don't have your miracle yet is because you don't have enough faith." Well, for me that's a no-brainer. Of course I don't have enough faith. Who ever had enough faith?

But I've got more faith than I had! Why do I say that? Because when I look where I was twenty years ago, and consider where I am today, I realize that I have more faith operating in my spirit today than I had twenty years ago. I'm being "strengthened in faith."

But I don't have as much faith as I'm going to have. Why do I say that? Because I'm being "strengthened in faith." I'm going to continue in this good fight of faith, regardless of the daily ups and downs. By God's grace, I will continue to grow in faith until I am "perfect and complete, lacking nothing."

One reason I'm talking about our ups and downs is because the accuser tries to use them against us. He whispers things like, "God really did give you some amazing promises, and He really was going to write a great story with your life; but you have pre-empted yourself from the storyline. You're too much of a basket case. You're a wreck. You have only yourself to blame. You've disqualified yourself from the story."

It's a lie. He just wants you to abort the story. Being a roller coaster does not disqualify you. What disqualifies you is if you abandon your trajectory.

Strengthen yourself again in His precious promises, stay in the story, and God will finish what He has started in your life.

Part Three: A Story of Biblical Proportions
TREACHERY, LOSS, DARKNESS, RESURRECTION

Most Mentioned Person

CHAPTER 12

In this final section, I want to tell a story—a story that graphically illustrates the glorious truths we've covered. In fact, I consider it to be one of the best stories in the Bible. And yet it is told rather rarely. If it's told, it's usually not from its most helpful perspective.

It's the story of the guy whose name appears most frequently in the Bible.

Here's how I think. I reckon that if someone's name appears a lot in the Bible, that points in an indirect way to the importance of their life. The connection may be loose, but there must be some kind of connection between the number of times a person's name is mentioned and the significance of their role in the cosmic story of redemption.

With that possibility in view, I did a word count on the names that appear most frequently in the Bible. I discovered that there are seven Bible characters whose names are mentioned over 300 times in the Bible.

Number seven in the list is Aaron. Aaron's name is mentioned 322 times because he was the first high priest in Moses' tabernacle. The frequent mentions are understandable because of his pivotal role in the launch of the tabernacle.

I'm not sure you want to be sixth on any Bible list, because six is considered to be the number of man. It's not always a complimentary number. For example, 666 is the number of the beast (Rev. 13:18). So who gets the number six slot? Saul, the first king of Israel. His name is mentioned 394 times.

Judah is fifth on the list. The name count jumps from Saul's 394 to Judah's 832. The royal line came from the tribe of Judah, hence the frequent mentions.

Coming in at number four is Moses. His name is mentioned 851 times, which is understandable considering Moses' primary role in guiding Israel out of Egypt and through the wilderness.

Coming in at number three? Jesus. It is certainly fitting that His name should appear 980 times in the Bible, for He is the very embodiment of our salvation and redemption.

Coming in at number two is David. Jesus was just under a thousand, and David is just over a thousand—at 1,087 mentions. His story is strategically central to the kingdom, so it seems quite reasonable that such an important figure would be mentioned so frequently.

Who holds the number one position? Interestingly, the count takes a sudden and unprecedented jump from around a thousand to nearly three thousand mentions. The man mentioned most frequently by name in the Bible is cited (surprise!) three times as frequently as Jesus. Jesus was at 980, but this man's count is 2,930.

When I tell you the man's name, you are going to think that I was being tricky with it. Because our leader was actually given two names in the Bible. His birth parents gave him the name Jacob, but then the Lord later gave him the name Israel. When you tally the occurrences of Jacob (363) and Israel (2,567) in the Bible, then add them together, you come up with 2,930 mentions. No one else comes close.

My point being, I think the guy is important.

In his psalms, David had a stronger fixation on Jacob than the other fathers. I share David's preoccupation.

To clarify, even though Jacob's name occurs three times more frequently than Jesus, I am not inferring that Jacob is three times more important than Christ. Never! Jesus alone is the cornerstone, the crucified Lamb, the head of the church, and the Lord of glory. I am simply pointing out that Jacob was more pivotal to the story-line of redemptive history than many people typically recognize.

Come with me, please, as we survey the life of one of the most colorful personalities in all of Scripture.

Two Brothers

CHAPTER 13

Jacob had a twin brother named Esau, and the rivalry between the two seemed to begin from birth. Esau was born first, but Jacob came out right behind him with his fingers wrapped around Esau's heel.

The competition only grew as they entered adulthood. As the firstborn, Esau naturally inherited the birthright. Perhaps the foremost benefit to the son with the birthright was that he inherited twice as much of the family inheritance as the other sons. Only a third of Isaac's possessions would fall to Jacob, therefore, whereas two-thirds would be Esau's. Jacob had his eye on the birthright, and finally found an opportunity to barter for it.

Esau came home from the field one day, weary and famished. When he saw that Jacob had made a savory stew, Esau asked his brother for a meal. Jacob took advantage of the opportunity and offered to give Esau food in exchange for the birthright.

In his depleted condition, Esau said, "Look, I am about to die; so what is this birthright to me?" (Gen. 25:32). So Esau swore by an oath to give Jacob the birthright in exchange for stew. Thus, Esau valued satisfying his bodily appetites over the benefits of the birthright.

But the rivalry was not over.

Thinking that he might die soon, Isaac decided it was time to bestow upon Esau the blessing due the firstborn son. He instructed Esau to hunt down an animal and prepare the meat so that he might eat and then bless him.

Overhearing the conversation, Rebekah quickly conceived of

a plan for Jacob to pretend to be Esau and to swindle the blessing from his father. She commanded Jacob to kill a couple young goats so that she might prepare a delicious meal. Isaac was blind due to age, so there was hope of fooling him. He could still touch, smell, and hear, though, so Rebekah needed a way to trick those three remaining senses that were still functioning.

How to get past Isaac's hearing? Jacob could muffle his voice as though he were affected by allergies or laryngitis. What about Isaac's ability to smell? Jacob could wear one of Esau's stinky garments. How about touch? She could put goat hair on Jacob's neck and arms to resemble Esau's hairy features. In this manner, she planned a way for Jacob to convince his father that he was Esau.

Jacob put on the garment and goat skin, took the meal to his father, and managed to get his blessing. Thus, he deceived his father into giving him a blessing befitting a firstborn.

I used to think that Jacob did all this because he was under his mother's influence. But then I did the math on Jacob's timeline. Do you know how old Jacob was when he pulled that stunt? Approximately seventy-five!

I don't think it was merely maternal influence. I think he knew what he was doing.

This makes us wonder what kind of a man Jacob truly was. Was he a shyster, a rascal, a conniving scoundrel? Was he a self-centered opportunist? Who was this man, really, at the core of his being?

The book of Psalms gives us the answer: "This is Jacob, the generation of those who seek Him, who seek Your face" (Ps. 24:6). This verse reveals that, in the essence of his person, Jacob was a seeker of God's face. He is representative of all those who seek after God. If you are a God-seeker, you have the heart of Jacob. Jacob had a zealous passion for his inheritance in God and he was willing to do whatever it took to get it.

"But," I can imagine someone complaining, "he didn't seek God right."

True. But neither did you. Not one of us has ever prayed the right prayer or cried the right cry in reaching out to God. We are incapable of seeking God in a perfect way. In fact, the book of Revelation reveals that God often directs angels to add incense to the prayers of His people (Rev. 8:3-4) because if the prayer would come to Him directly without the added "sweetener" of incense, it would irritate Him so much that it might possibly be dismissed.

Jacob embodies the inadequacy of us all to pursue God properly. And he also embodies the kindness and mercy of God to look past our inadequacies, see the sincere reach of our hearts, and reward us with the favor of His countenance. We don't get anything from God because we prayed the right prayer; we receive from God because His mercy is as vast as the universe (Ps. 36:5).

Jacob got where he did because God had mercy on him.

Vessel of Mercy

In fact, Jacob is one of the most quintessential examples in the entire Bible of an object of mercy. When I say "object of mercy," I am borrowing the language of Romans 9:22-23, where it describes two kinds of people in the earth: those who are vessels of God's wrath and those who are vessels of His mercy. God chose to make Jacob a vessel of mercy, and the profusion of mercy on his life was really quite remarkable.

Before I develop that thought, let me back up a bit and define mercy. When we grasp the nature of mercy, its presence in Jacob's life becomes all the more meaningful.

Mercy and grace are sometimes lumped together, but they are not the same thing. One of the common ways to distinguish them is with these definitions:

"Mercy is God not giving me what I deserve."

"Grace is God giving me what I do not deserve."

Those definitions are accurate, but they do not fully represent the depth of the two concepts. The meaning of mercy blossoms when we view it as defined by its first occurrence in the Bible. The "law of first mention" is a principle of biblical interpretation that suggests the first mention of a word or concept in the Bible sets a precedent, defining and shaping how that word is to be understood throughout Scripture.

"Mercy" first appears in the Bible in the story of Lot.

When the morning dawned, the angels urged Lot to hurry, saying, "Arise, take your wife and your two daughters who are here, lest you be consumed in the punishment of the city." And while he lingered, the men took hold of his hand, his wife's hand, and the hands of his two daughters, the LORD being merciful to him, *and they brought him out and set him outside the city. So it came to pass, when they had brought them outside, that he said, "Escape for your life! Do not look behind you nor stay any-where in the plain. Escape to the mountains, lest you be destroyed."* (Gen. 19:15-17).

Notice how God showed His mercy to Lot. The angels grabbed his hand and those of his household and led—yes, cor-ralled and almost dragged—them out of the city of Sodom.

Lot would not have left the city in his own power. It's not that he rebelled against the Lord's command to flee the city's destruc-tion. He was simply obtuse. Dull. Thick-skulled. Hard-hearted. Oblivious. The warning of the angels was not penetrating his cog-nitive powers. He was lingering because of foggy bewilderment. So the Lord had mercy on him. An angel grabbed his hand and mercifully led him on a course that would save his life.

Based on this incident, I have come to appreciate this defini-tion of mercy: Mercy is the kindness of God to get you going in the way you need to go, in spite of yourself.

Mercy gets you pointed in the right direction. *Grace* gives you the strength and momentum to move forward in the right direction.

I am so grateful that God has made me a vessel of mercy. That means He is constantly and recurrently recalibrating my course and getting me back on track—even though in weakness and bro-kenness I often digress. What glorious mercy! And how desper-ately I need it.

We see this kind of mercy demonstrated frequently toward Jacob. In fact, Psalm 24 (quoted earlier) shows just how merciful God was to Jacob. Look at it again.

Who may ascend into the hill of the LORD? Or who may stand in His holy place? He who has clean hands and a pure heart, who has not lifted up his soul to an idol, nor sworn deceitfully. He shall receive blessing from the LORD, and righteousness from the God of his salva-tion. This is Jacob, the generation of those who seek Him, who seek Your face. Selah (Ps. 24:3-6).

Because Jacob sought the face of God, God brought him into the hill of the Lord. Jacob stood in the holy place.

Yet, when we look at the qualifications for standing before God, Jacob blew three of the four qualifications. We are told that the one who would stand in the holy place must meet four requirements:

1. *He must have clean hands.*

   Well, Jacob blew that one. He had bloodied goat skin on his hands when he tricked his father into believing he was Esau. He flunked the first test.

2. *He must have a pure heart.*

   Well, Jacob certainly did not meet that standard. Would a man with a pure heart take advantage of his brother's famished condition and coerce him into selling his birthright for the sake of a meal?

3. *He must not lift up his soul to an idol.*

   Well, at least we have one qualification that Jacob did not violate. There is no record in Scripture that he ever nodded to an idol.

4. *He must not swear deceitfully.*

   Jacob blew that one big time! He blatantly lied to his father, "I am Esau." It would be difficult to find a clearer example in Scripture of swearing deceitfully.

Jacob failed three of the four qualifications for standing in the presence of God, and yet God was merciful to him and brought him into His presence.

Why? Because He loved the fact that Jacob, at the very core of his being, wanted God Himself.

Jacob's story testifies powerfully to the mercy of God. Left to himself, Jacob would not have gotten even close to his divine destiny. God mercifully intervened and led him into His holy place.

Interestingly, God's mercy is attracted toward those we would naturally consider most unlikely. Esau seemed to be the more fitting candidate, but it was Jacob who received mercy. And the apostle Paul, as another example, claimed to receive mercy specifically because he sinned more than anyone else, in blatant ignorance and unbelief. (See 1 Tim. 1:13-16.)

Mercy is given to those who deserve it least. That certainly is good news for us!

DID JACOB STEAL THE BLESSING?

I used to think that Jacob stole Esau's blessing. However, that's not how God viewed it. Here is how the Holy Spirit interpreted that event:

> Lest there be any fornicator or profane person like Esau, who for one morsel of food sold his birthright. For you know that afterward, when he wanted to inherit the blessing, he was rejected, for he found no place for repentance, though he sought it diligently with tears (Heb. 12:16-17).

This passage does not say that Jacob stole Esau's blessing. It says God *rejected* Esau from receiving it.

God could have easily given Esau an equally great blessing, but Isaac's spirit shriveled when he tried to bless Esau. Isaac could not give to Esau what the Spirit was not giving. In contrast, when blessing Jacob, the Spirit of prophecy surged within Isaac's soul.

No man can steal the blessing God has for you.

I cannot imagine what happens within the soul of the person who realizes, "God has rejected me." All the souls in hell know this feeling. Rejected by God. Horrifying!

In contrast, Jacob was accepted by God—not because he was less sinful than Esau, but because he yearned for God.

What does the verse mean when it says Esau "found no place for repentance"? Instead of recognizing the apathy of his heart and repenting for it, he could only see Jacob's fault and blame his brother. His tears were not tears of repentance for his own sin, but of anger and frustration at his brother's sin. Esau saw himself as a victim, not a sinner. Even though he sought the blessing with tears, he was rejected by God because he had no repentance.

We conclude, therefore, that even though Jacob deceived his father, he did not receive Esau's blessing. Rather, he received the blessing that God had in His heart for him alone.

LOVED AND HATED

Why did the Lord say, "Jacob I have loved; but Esau I have hated" (Mal. 1:2-3)? Did the Lord love Jacob because he was such a nice guy, but hate Esau because he was a surly jerk? No, it was not like that at all. Alan Vincent, in his excellent book, *The Good Fight of Faith*, suggests that, on the merit of raw personality, Esau was the more likeable man. God's choices are not based upon "likeability," however, but upon what He sees in the heart.

Jacob had a passionate yearning for God, and God loved that about him. In contrast, Esau was indifferent toward his spiritual inheritance, and I believe that is what God hated about Esau.

In practical terms, how was that love and hatred expressed? What did it mean to be loved or hated by God?

Here is how God demonstrated His love for Jacob: He fastened His gaze on him. God took an active, keen interest in every aspect of Jacob's life. The day would come when Jacob would limp because of that divine attention.

And here is how God demonstrated His hatred for Esau: He simply left Esau alone.

Being under the gaze of God is incredibly intense! David wanted God's attention, so he prayed, "Look upon me and be merciful to me" (Ps. 119:132)[1]. Then, when he got the gaze of God, it was much more fiery than he was expecting, so he changed his tune and implored, "Remove Your gaze from me...before I go away and am no more" (Ps. 39:13). Job said it this way, "Will You not look away from me, and let me alone till I swallow my saliva?" (Job 7:19).

Being loved by God—being under His gaze—was actually very troubling for Jacob. That gaze meant he was hounded by heaven all his days. As a result, he experienced many trials and sorrows. (See Genesis 47:9.)

When you look at Esau's life, the contrast is striking. His was "the blessed life." Esau had wives, children, grandchildren, protection, honor, stability, friends, good fortune, abundance, and serenity. Based on externals, Esau appeared to be living under divine favor. He was established, settled in his own land, and surrounded by his posterity in peace and quiet.

Why was Esau's life marked by such tranquility and prosperity? Because God left him alone. Why was Jacob's life marked by such affliction and trial? Because God would not get off his case.

So there are basically two choices for us: to be under the gaze

1 Some ascribe Psalm 119 to David's pen, but no one knows for sure who wrote it.

of God, or to be ignored by Him.

Being under divine scrutiny is extremely rigorous. The only thing worse is divine indifference.

Lord, I realize I do not fully understand the implications of what I am about to say, but nevertheless here is my simple prayer. Do not leave me alone. Do not leave me to my own devices and ways. Interrupt my life, set Your gaze upon me, and lead me into Your mercy and truth. Love me like You loved Jacob!

Bethel's Vow
CHAPTER 14

Esau held a bitter grudge against Jacob because of the blessing Jacob had deceitfully gotten from his father. He quietly resolved in his heart that, once his father had died, he would kill Jacob.

Aware of his brother's animosity, Jacob decided to move away until his brother's anger had subsided. Under the direction of his parents, he embarked on a trek for his uncle Laban's house in Haran.

By this time, Esau had been married to two wives for thirty-five years, but Jacob was still single and approximately seventy-five years old. He was hoping to find a good wife from among Laban's relatives.

On his journey, he stopped for the night in a place that would later be named Bethel. He found a smooth stone to use for a pillow.

That night he had a dream of a ladder reaching from earth to heaven, with angels ascending and descending on it. The Lord stood at the top of the ladder and spoke to Jacob.

I am the LORD God of Abraham your father and the God of Isaac; the land on which you lie I will give to you and your descendants. Also your descendants shall be as the dust of the earth; you shall spread abroad to the west and the east, to the north and the south; and in you and in your seed all the families of the earth shall be blessed. Behold, I am with you and will keep you wherever you go, and will bring you back to this land; for I will not leave you until I have done what I have spoken to you (Gen. 28:13-15).

Notice that He was not yet the God of Jacob. He introduced

Himself to Jacob as the God of his fathers Abraham and Isaac, but He did not presume to be Jacob's God.

Then the Lord made a series of promises to Jacob that we recognize as the same promises made to Abraham. God was assuring Jacob that he, not Esau, would inherit the blessings promised to Abraham.

Then the Lord said, "I will not leave you until I have done what I have spoken to you." He was assuring Jacob that while the promise was delayed, He Himself would be at Jacob's side until it came to pass.

Presence accompanies promise. Whenever God gives a promise, He always attends it with His presence. His presence preserves and protects the promise until it is fulfilled.

In response to the Lord's marvelous assurance, Jacob made a vow.

There are different kinds of vows in the Bible. One kind is a conditional vow, which promises to do certain things if God will do certain things. A conditional vow often sounds something like this: "God, if You will answer my prayer, then I will do such-and-such."

One of the most famous biblical vows along this line is the vow of Hannah. She vowed to the Lord that, if He would grant her a son, she would give him back to Him. He took her up on it. He gave her Samuel, and she was good to her vow—she gave him back to God. (See 1 Samuel 1.)

Similarly, Jacob made a conditional vow to the Lord.

> Then Jacob made a vow, saying, "If God will be with me, and keep me in this way that I am going, and give me bread to eat and clothing to put on, so that I come back to my father's house in peace, then the LORD shall be my God" (Gen. 28:20-21).

Jacob had a list of conditions. "God, if You will do this, this, this, this, and this, then You shall be my God." Jacob was affirming that the God of his fathers was not yet his God. However, if God would meet the conditions of his vow, then Jacob would seal a covenant with Him.

Uttering this vow constituted one of the most pivotal moments in Jacob's life. The rest of his story revolved around the confirmation of this vow and its implications. Here we go.

Peniel

CHAPTER 15

Jacob's next twenty years were spent in Haran with his uncle Laban's family. Here is a quick summary of what happened during that time.

- Jacob fell in love with Laban's younger daughter, Rachel, and agreed to work for seven years for her hand in marriage.
- He was tricked by Laban into marrying his oldest daughter, Leah, instead.
- Jacob worked an additional seven years so he could have Rachel. Thus, he served Laban fourteen years for both daughters.
- Later, he married Leah's maid, Zilpah, and Rachel's maid, Bilhah.
- In less than thirteen years, Jacob fathered eleven sons by four wives.
- After serving Laban for fourteen years, the two men came to a new arrangement. Jacob would continue to shepherd Laban's flocks and his wages would be all the spotted, speckled, and brown animals in the flock.
- Jacob became wealthy in short order with large flocks, servants, camels, and donkeys.
- After twenty years in Haran, and being ninety-five years old, Jacob returned to Canaan. Fearing that his father-in-law

would not release him freely, Jacob stole away unannounced. Laban caught up to him ten days later, at which time they made a pact to do each other no harm.

After the agreement with Laban, Jacob continued on his way toward Canaan, coming eventually to a place called Peniel. Peniel was located a few miles east of the Jordan, just shy of Canaan proper. Jacob named the place Peniel, "face of God," because of the encounter he had there.

As Jacob approached Canaan, God came collecting on the vow Jacob had made twenty years earlier. At Peniel, God was essentially saying, "Ante up." It's as though God was thinking, "When you left Canaan, you said that if I would do this, this, this, this, and this, then I would be your God. Well, I've done all those things. How about it, Jacob? Will you deliver on the vow you made? Am I now your God?"

The biblical account of the encounter at Peniel begins like this: "Then Jacob was left alone; and a Man wrestled with him until the breaking of day" (Gen. 32:24). God arranged for Jacob to be left alone so He could meet with him. (Loneliness is sometimes a setup for encounter.) In the New King James Version, the word "Man" in this verse is capitalized. That is because most scholars concur that the Man wrestling with Jacob on this occasion must have been the Son of God in a pre-incarnate form. It was Jesus Himself.

Now when He saw that He did not prevail against him, He touched the socket of his hip; and the socket of Jacob's hip was out of joint as He wrestled with him. And He said, "Let Me go, for the day breaks." But he said, "I will not let You go unless You bless me!" So He said to him, "What is your name?" He said, "Jacob." And He said, "Your name shall no longer be called Jacob, but Israel; for you have struggled with God and with men, and have prevailed." Then Jacob asked, saying, "Tell me Your name, I pray." And He said, "Why is it that you ask about My name?" And He blessed him there. So Jacob called the name of the place Peniel: "For I have seen God face to face, and my life is preserved." Just as he crossed over Penuel the sun rose on him, and he limped on his hip. Therefore to this day the children of Israel do not eat the muscle that shrank, which is on the hip socket, because He touched the socket of Jacob's hip in the muscle that shrank (Gen. 32:25-32).

Obviously, Jesus allowed Jacob to prevail against Him. Jesus could have leveled Jacob, but He restrained Himself. He came in a form that Jacob could overcome, but it would require every reserve of strength within his frame to do so.

As they wrestled, Jesus reached out His hand—the hand that we so often associate with touching the blind and they see, touching the lame and they leap, touching the deaf and they hear, touching the dead and they rise—Jesus stretched forth *that* hand and *wounded* Jacob. He shrank the muscle on the hip socket.

Muscles support all the bone sockets in our bodies, keeping the bones in place in their sockets. When Jesus touched the hip socket muscle, He neutralized the ability of that muscle to keep the hip in its socket. Now, the hip was prone to come out of socket with just normal, everyday hip movement.

As long as the hip was in socket, Jacob could function okay. Whatever discomfort he might have felt was minimal and manageable. What was unmanageable was when the hip went out of socket. When that bone came out, it was like someone drove a knife through his hip. The pain was instantaneous and excruciating.

Perhaps you have experienced something similar to Jacob. Perhaps you had a sports injury, or some other type of accident, that caused a bone in your body to go out of socket. All you could think about was, *Get the bone back in socket!* In some cases, you may still have a weakness in that joint and if you move it in the wrong way, it may come out of socket again. If your injury has the propensity to recur, you will guard that joint very carefully because of the searing pain that accompanies recurrence. That is what it was like for Jacob.

After this wounding, Jacob didn't limp because it hurt to walk; he limped because he was constantly favoring that joint. He could not afford for it to go out of socket. The pain was too intense. So every step became a calculated rigmarole to keep that hip in its socket. To nurse it, he had to slow his pace and adjust the way he swung his legs forward. It required a limp.

WRESTLING IN PAIN

We are told that Jacob's hip was out of socket *while he was wrestling with Jesus.* Not only was Jacob in agonizing pain because the thing was out of socket, he was fighting for his life at the same time.

Every movement in the tussle was pressing on those raw nerves.

The flashes of agony would be similar to someone putting a nail through your feet, and then making you stand on the nail. The injury itself is excruciating enough, but now it feels like dozens of knives are being driven into the wound.

Jesus, what gives You the right to dish out this kind of pain? Do You even know what this feels like? Do You know what it's like to have Your bones out of joint, and then to writhe on those joints?[1]

Hosea gave us an interesting window into this wrestling match. He added this comment about Jacob while in the struggle: "He wept, and sought favor from Him" (Hos. 12:4). Hosea told us something Genesis didn't: Jacob was weeping during this encounter.

Did Jacob weep because the pain was so severe, or because he wanted God so badly? In the distress of the ordeal, I doubt Jacob could separate it out. "I don't know if I'm crying because I'm hurting so intensely, or if I'm crying because I want You and Your blessing so badly. All I know is, I'm in so much pain and I want You so desperately!"

Even if you can't distinguish why you're weeping, don't toughen up and resist. Covet tears. Tears are liquid prayer. Just as the nectar of squeezed fruit is sweet, so the tears that come from a crushed heart are sweet to God. Do not despise the thing He uses to unlock your fountain of tears. Often the thing needed is pain.

"But pain is not of God," someone might argue.

Tell that to Jacob.

THE PAIN OF HOLDING ON

Jacob found himself in a position where holding onto God became his more painful option. It would have been easier to let go. His body was telling him, "Let the Man go and tend to your hip." But something else was insisting from within, "I will never let go until He blesses me."

You can find yourself in a situation where holding to God is more painful than letting go. And the unfortunate truth is that some people let go.

1 Yes, that is exactly how Jesus suffered. David spoke of His suffering when he wrote, "I am poured out like water, and all My bones are out of joint" (Ps. 22:14).

Something gets out of joint for them. Something goes wrong, whether it be relational or financial or physical. Their pain shoots through the roof, and holding to God only adds more distress. In the struggle of the darkness and perplexity, they let go of God.

May that alternative never come near my soul. I have asked the Lord to give me the spirit of Jacob. "Jesus, place in me the tenacity and resolve of Jacob to hold on to You, regardless of the distress. By Your grace, I will not let go until You bless me!"

HOLDING ON TO PROMISE

Now that Jacob had Promise in his grip, he was not about to let go. I say he had Promise in his grip because Promise is a Person. The Holy Spirit is called "the Promise of the Father" (Acts 1:4), indicating that Promise is a Person. When you have your fingers wrapped around Promise, you have hold of a piece of God.

Jacob was holding on to Promise Himself, and Promise was pushing Jacob away, saying, "Let Me go!" (Gen. 32:26).

When you have a promise from God, that promise will take on a life of its own and try to break free of your grip. The longer you are holding onto a promise, the more it will try to get away from you. Holding on to promise long-term is a colossal challenge.

Speaking from personal experience, as I have held to my promise of healing, I can't count the number of times promise has tried to get away from me. But by the grace of God, my heart is steadfast; I am resolved to do whatever is necessary to hold on to my promise and stay in faith.

May the spirit of Jacob be ours! We will never let go of You, Jesus, until You answer the cry of our hearts.

Spiritual Fatherhood

CHAPTER 16

God did not take down Jacob's ability to hold on; He took down his ability to push. He did not hit Jacob in the shoulder; He hit him in the hip.

The legs of a man represent his ability to push. When you want a job done, do not give it to an old man whose strength has been broken, give it to a young man with young legs. A young man will strap himself to a project, position his legs under him, and then push his way to completion.

Jacob was the kind of man you wanted around when there was work to do. He was a can-do guy. When he wanted to accomplish something, he would gather his legs under him and push until the thing was done. When Jacob had his sights on a goal, you had better get out of his way or he might run you over.

Jacob was a pusher. He pushed his way into the birthright; he pushed his way into the blessing; and he pushed his way into gaining his father-in-law's flocks and herds.

When God visited Jacob to break his strength, He strategically took down his ability to push. Why? Because, as the Scripture says, "He takes no pleasure in the legs of a man" (Ps. 147:10). God does not delight in watching a man muster his natural strengths and abilities, and then throw himself headlong into the acquisition of his objective. God had watched Jacob push his way through life and it wasn't doing anything for Him.

Broken Strength

God's response was to make Jacob unable to push. With a wrecked hip, he was rendered physically incapable of ramming his way through life.

"Sorry," I can imagine him saying to a friend, "But if you have a project that requires strong legs, you're going to have to get someone else. I simply can't do it."

Every step became extremely tentative and guarded. He had to watch how quickly he walked and how he tried to change directions. One careless move and *pop!* the socket would be out, and he would be on the ground—writhing. The injury forced him to find a new way of walking.

The legs of a man bring God no pleasure, but there is a way of laboring that *does* give His heart pleasure. It is described in Zechariah 4:6. "'Not by might nor by power, but by My Spirit,' says the LORD of hosts." God is pleased when we tap into the power of the Holy Spirit to accomplish His purposes, and this is what He wanted for Jacob. In order for him to find this way, though, God had to remove the props that kept him tethered to his natural abilities. When God disabled his natural strength, it opened the way for him to become a deeply spiritual man.

What was God after in Jacob? In one word, meekness. Meekness is the character quality God develops in your spirit when He takes your hip out.

Meekness is the opposite of pushing. A pusher says, "Get out of my way or I'll run you over." Meekness does not handle people in a rough manner because it relies on the strength of Christ to obtain its objective. Meekness is strength administered in gentleness. You're struck not by the person's strength, but their humility.

Meekness can be mistaken for weakness by the casual observer, but it is far from wimpy; it is strong in the grace and power of Jesus.

Meekness has to do with your fathering paradigm. Let me explain.

Jacob's Fathering Paradigm

Prior to Peniel, Jacob fathered his children in the manner that came most naturally to him. He pushed. He was just being himself.

His sons grew up watching a self-determining pusher as he made his way forward in life.

Peniel was the place where God infused Jacob with meekness so that he could parent Joseph effectively. Peniel was not as much about Jacob as it was about Joseph. Peniel was the place where God changed Jacob so he could get His Joseph.

Peniel—the place where God changed Jacob's name and gave him a limp—was all about changing his fathering paradigm. Why? Because Jacob's track record as a pusher-father was not so good. Take a look, for example, at Jacob's four eldest sons.

- Reuben: The day would come when he would sleep with one of his father's wives.
- Simeon and Levi: They were hot-heads. Their anger was cruel. In their anger, they would one day destroy an entire community of people.
- Judah: He would eventually consort with a prostitute—and if he did it once without remorse, who's to say it was his only time?

Looking at where Jacob's sons were headed, I imagine God thinking, "Jacob, this is not going in a good direction. The way you are fathering your children right now is not producing a godly generation. If I leave you to yourself, I will never get My Joseph."

God came and interrupted Jacob's life while Joseph was approximately four years old (give or take). Joseph was still in his formative years. God wanted to change Jacob while the cement of Joseph's young heart was still pliable and impressionable.

The brothers were raised by Jacob; Joseph was raised by Israel.

When God chooses a Joseph generation, He starts by changing the fathers and mothers. He takes down the hips of His Jacobs, infusing them with meekness, that they might raise up a noble Joseph generation in the earth.

INTER-GENERATIONAL CONNECTIVITY

The connection between Jacob and Joseph is fascinating, depicted in a unique way in Genesis 37.

> *Now Jacob dwelt in the land where his father was a stranger, in the*
> *land of Canaan. This is the history of Jacob. Joseph, being seventeen*
> *years old, was feeding the flock with his brothers (Gen.* 37:1-2).

Look again at the second verse. "This is the history of Jacob. Joseph..." Did I see that correctly? Look at it again. "This is the history of Jacob. Joseph..."

Wait a minute. Whose history are we talking about here? Are we telling Jacob's story or Joseph's story?

The answer is, Jacob's. Moses (the author of Genesis) realized that when he launched into Joseph's saga, most readers would assume that Jacob's story was over and that he had moved on to Joseph's story. Moses did not want us to make that mistake, so he gave us an editorial tip, "This is the history of Jacob." He was telling us, "Even though I am writing about Joseph, I am still on Jacob's story."

Why? Because Joseph's story *is* Jacob's story. Jacob's story will be incomplete unless Joseph enters into his destiny. Here is the takeaway point: *The stories of successive generations are intrinsically bound up together.*

I want you to see how Joseph's and Jacob's destinies were bound up together.

Initially, Jacob set up Joseph for greatness. But then look how the story ended. By the time it was done, *Joseph set up Jacob for greatness.* Joseph brought his father to Pharaoh and said, "Papa, I'd like you to meet Pharaoh. Pharaoh, I'd like you to meet my papa." Then Jacob stretched out his soul and blessed Pharaoh (Gen. 47:7-10). Thus, before his death, Jacob blessed the most powerful man on the planet. And we know the principle of Hebrews 7:7,[1] that the lesser is blessed by the better.

Jacob went out the best man on earth! And the only reason he finished in such greatness is because of Joseph. Joseph had to ascend to the palace so that he could position his father for greatness.

Eventually, the whole thing came full circle, ending with Jacob's regal finish. Joseph's story was Jacob's story after all.

At the time of this writing, my children are in their twenties. When your children get into their twenties or older, it can

---

1   "Now beyond all contradiction the lesser is blessed by the better" (Heb. 7:7).

be tempting for parents to think, "I've done my best. I've trained them up in the way they should go. I've prepared them for life I've poured my best into them. There comes a time when they have to find their own wings. They've got to make their own way in life. I guess it's time for me to let go, so they can find their own way forward."

But when you understand the Jacob/Joseph bond, you gain a godly jealousy for something you're not willing to lose. You realize that how your children run their race directly affects the outcome of your race. Let them go? Never! I'm holding on more resolutely than ever. I am contending for them to enter into the fullness of their upward calling in Christ.

Marked by God

When God compromised Jacob's hip and reduced him to a limp, the encounter left an indelible imprint on his life. Everybody could see the difference in him ever after. Even those who were too dull to discern the inward change could not help but see the change in Jacob's walk.

Everyone was talking about the change.

I can imagine Joseph's friends asking him, "Joseph, why does your dad limp?"

"He has walked like that," I suppose Joseph responding, "ever since He met with God."

The change in Jacob had a profound effect upon his children. It also had a striking impact on his brother, Esau. When Jacob and Esau were reunited, their meeting took place less than twenty-four hours after Jacob's hip injury. Jacob had not even begun to heal up from the encounter with Christ.

Now Jacob lifted his eyes and looked, and there, Esau was coming, and with him were four hundred men. So he divided the children among Leah, Rachel, and the two maidservants. And he put the maidservants and their children in front, Leah and her children behind, and Rachel and Joseph last. Then he crossed over before them and bowed himself to the ground seven times, until he came near to his brother. But Esau ran to meet him, and embraced him, and fell on his neck and kissed him, and they wept (Gen. 33:1-4).

As Jacob approached Esau and bowed to the ground seven times, he did it with an especially strong limp. His wound was fresh and the pain biting. Considering the contorted movements Jacob had to employ to keep the hip in joint, falling on the ground and getting up seven times must have made for a pitiful sight.

It seems that the visual impact of watching his limping brother fall on the ground and get up repeatedly in such a condition helped to produce a change of heart within Esau. When they finally embraced, Esau's heart was soft and accepting. Jacob was marked by God, and now he was leaving a mark on all those around him.

The Altar at Shechem

CHAPTER 17

Jacob's reconciliation with Esau took place on the east side of the Jordan. After their parting, he continued his westward progress.

Coming to the Jordan, Israel helped his family and flocks make the crossing. Once he had traversed the Jordan, he stepped foot in Canaan—his first time in twenty years. It was an emotional homecoming.

The first place he set up camp was in a town called Shechem. And the first thing that he did in Shechem is very noteworthy. Now that he was actually back in Canaan proper, he had some business to tend to. An altar needed to be built and a transaction settled.

Then he erected an altar there and called it El Elohe Israel (Gen. 33:20).

This altar at Shechem was a watershed moment for Israel. The significance of the altar is seen in the meaning of its name. He called the altar El Elohe Israel, the interpretation of those Hebrew words being, "God, the God of Israel."

At this altar, Israel was declaring, "God is now my God. He is now the God of Israel."

Recall the history behind that statement. Twenty years earlier, God had identified Himself as the God of Abraham and the God of Isaac. But He did not claim to be the God of Jacob. At the time, Jacob made a vow with God, saying that if God would meet certain conditions, then He would be his God. Now, twenty years later, the conditions were met. God had protected and blessed

Jacob and had returned him to Canaan.

Shechem is the place where Jacob confirmed the vow. At this altar, Jacob was saying, "You are now my God. I will serve you all my days. No matter what happens from this moment forward, You will always be my God."

It is here, at Shechem, that He became the God of Abraham, and the God of Isaac, and the God of Jacob. The covenant was sealed.

It is easy to be critical of Jacob, but I will say this to his credit. He never turned away from the vow that he sealed at Shechem. Once he came into covenant and made the God of his fathers his own God, he never backed away or relented from that covenant. He served God through thick and thin until his death.

And my, how that covenant was about to be tested!

Losing Joseph

CHAPTER 18

One day, when Jacob was 108 years old, the ten oldest brothers came to their father with a garment in hand that was bloodied and torn. They had sold their brother Joseph into slavery, mangled his clothes to resemble an attack from a wild beast, and then brought the tunic to their father. They asked their father if he recognized the garment. Naturally, he did. It was the coat of many colors that Jacob had made especially for his most beloved son, Joseph.

> And he recognized it and said, "It is my son's tunic. A wild beast has devoured him. Without doubt Joseph is torn to pieces." Then Jacob tore his clothes, put sackcloth on his waist, and mourned for his son many days. And all his sons and all his daughters arose to comfort him; but he refused to be comforted, and he said, "For I shall go down into the grave to my son in mourning." Thus his father wept for him (Gen. 37:33-35).

The loss of Joseph catapulted Jacob into an abyss of sorrow and grief. The depth of Jacob's grief almost seems excessive. Why would he resolve to mourn Joseph's passing to the day of his death? I see two reasons.

First, Joseph was his favorite son, and he missed him terribly. But I think the second reason was the stronger.

Jacob was a prophet. We see this clearly in the way he spoke over the destiny and future of each of his sons near the time of his death. (See Genesis 48-49.) He spoke to them as a prophet, blessing each son according to the insight he had received from the Holy Spirit for them. Although the Bible does not explicitly say it, it's clear that Jacob knew Joseph was special. (See Genesis 37:11.) He may not have known, when Joseph was young, everything that God had in store for him, but he knew that the hand of God was upon this boy in an unusual way. Joseph was destined for greatness, and Jacob knew it by the Spirit.

When Jacob lost Joseph, he simply could not do the math. He could not reconcile his prophetic impressions with the fact that Joseph was now dead. The mix of perplexity and grief was so overwhelming to him that he said, "Do not even try to comfort me over this one. I will take this to my grave. I will never let go of my sorrow." And for twenty-two years Jacob refused to be comforted.

REFUSING TO BE COMFORTED

I relate to Jacob in a small way over his refusal to be comforted. His refusal reminds me of one of my favorite verses in the psalms, "My soul refused to be comforted" (Ps. 77:2). This verse means a lot to me because I know what it's like, when holding a promise from God, for a thousand voices to try to talk you into accepting a lesser settlement than the high road of God's complete promise. It's as though the voices want us to "dumb down" our request of God, to make it a little easier for Him to meet the conditions.

I refuse to accept second best in order to relieve God of the pressure of having to come through with a bell-ringing miracle. I am more inclined toward Elijah's approach. Dig a trench, douse the sacrifice with water, and fill the trench with water (1 Ki. 18:33-35). Make it even *more* difficult for God to deliver!

While I continue to wait on God to heal my throat (which I talked about in chapter five), here are a couple ways in which Psalm 77:2 is relevant to me.

Occasionally, after I have spoken somewhere in my low-muttering manner, people will say to me, "Bob, speaking as you do in this weakened condition actually works *for* you. It's an asset. People have to stop, tune their ears, and listen very attentively to hear what you have to say. People listen better to you than if you were yelling at them. The effect your voice has, in its broken condition, is that people listen more carefully to you than to most other preachers. This condition actually makes you more effective in your communication."

Well, I am grateful that God can use my small voice, even in
its weakened state. I am grateful that God can somehow use my
pain and weakness to make a stronger imprint on the hearts of
people. I am thankful that God is using my voice even now, during
this season, while I wait for His healing. But my soul refuses to be
comforted by this! I will not be comforted by anything less than
the fullness of His promised healing and deliverance.

Others have asked me, "Bob, if you had not suffered this injury to your voice, would you have written all the books you've
authored?" My answer is an immediate no. No way. Why not?
Because prior to the vocal injury, I was too busy to write books.
And I didn't have anything to say.

"Well, see then," they say, "Look how God has used this injury.
Your voice is going further in the earth now, through your writ-
ings, than when you had a voice. So it was actually a blessing that
God took your voice down."

Here is how I feel about that. I am grateful that God has been
able to use the greatest trial of my life to gain glory for His name.
I am so thankful for every book that is read and for every ounce
of encouragement that comes to the body of Christ through my
writing. But my soul refuses to be comforted by that. I refuse to be
comforted with anything less than the fullness of God's promise to
me. I will never be comforted until He opens the gates and releases
me.

Jacob was in a similar frame in his soul. He was immersed in
grief and no amount of talk would make him okay with the fact
that Joseph and his divine destiny had been stripped from him.
He refused to make peace with the loss. For twenty-two years he
mourned Joseph.

JACOB AT AGE 130

Jacob lost Joseph at age 108. Then we enter a twenty-two-year
period of silence in Jacob's story. We hear nothing of Jacob during those years because Moses (the author of Genesis) was totally
taken up with the story of Joseph. Moses had Joseph in the pit,
sold to the Ishmaelites, dragged to Egypt, sold on the slave block,
in Potiphar's house, sent to prison, and then promoted to the palace. Then Moses took us through seven plentiful years followed by

two years of famine. By the time we eventually catch up with Jacob again, twenty-two years had elapsed.

Jacob is now 130 years old. Count them. 1-3-0. Would you agree that he is now a mature elder in the faith? He has persevered in faithfulness ever since he sealed the covenant with God some thirty-five years earlier in Shechem. Tough to get a whole lot more mature than this.

And how do we find this great elder of the faith at age 130? Do we find him living in abundance, prosperity, happiness, and contentment? Do we find him emotionally fulfilled and self-actualized? Quite the opposite. Jacob was engulfed in blackness and distress. He had no idea what God was doing in his life nor where God was taking him.

If you are in a season of blackness, and have no idea what God is saying right now or where He is taking you, it may not necessarily be an indication of spiritual immaturity. Sometimes God turns the lights out to intensify the drama of the story.

Here's the background to Jacob's blackness. A prolonged, crushing drought had settled upon the land. It struck Jacob and his family with vehemence, devastating all the crops. When he heard that food could be purchased in Egypt, Jacob sent his ten oldest sons to buy some. When they got there, they didn't realize that the man selling Egypt's grain was their brother, Joseph. He recognized them, but they did not recognize him. He pretended to suspect them of being spies. Incarcerating Simeon in prison—the prison he himself had once inhabited—he sent the other brothers home with their food. He left them strict instructions that they dare not return for more food without their youngest brother, Benjamin, in tow.

So when we meet up with Jacob at age 130, the brothers had returned to Canaan, Simeon was left behind in an Egyptian prison, the food they brought back from Egypt was mostly consumed, and the brothers were putting pressure on their father to allow them to return to Egypt to buy more food. But to do so, they must take Benjamin with them.

Jacob was a seasoned father in the faith but he couldn't see past his nose, and his soul was overwhelmed with distress and pain. "I have lost my Joseph. I have lost my Simeon to the man in Egypt. And now the man in Egypt wants my Benjamin. I will *never* give him my Benjamin! Over my dead body will he get my Benjamin."

His sons tried to talk some sense to him. "Papa, it just may be over your dead body, because this famine is strangling our supply of food. If you don't relent, both you and your entire family are going to die of starvation."

"I can't lose Benjamin. I *won't* lose Benjamin!"

But they kept pressuring him because they needed more food. "Papa, are you willing for all your grandchildren to die of starvation, just so you can preserve Benjamin's life? Is that all we mean to you?"

Jacob couldn't stomach the loss of Benjamin, but neither could he allow the starvation of his family. Torn between the two, his distress levels became unbearable. The Bible gives us a glimpse into the duress Jacob was feeling:

> *And Jacob their father said to them, "You have bereaved me: Joseph is no more, Simeon is no more, and you want to take Benjamin. All these things are against me" (Gen. 42:36).*

I especially like the way the New International Version renders the last sentence in that verse: "Everything is against me!" That phrase captures Jacob's emotional state in this moment.

"I have lost my Joseph. And now I have lost my Simeon to the man in Egypt. What did I do to the man in Egypt? Why has he declared war on me? But that's not all, I have heaven against me, too." (The cause of a famine rests ultimately with the one who controls the weather—God.) "This confounded famine is sucking the life out of my family. Egypt is against me; God is against me; *everything* is against me!"

With this great, guttural cry, Jacob collapsed in a heap of abject helplessness. His only option was to let go and release everything to God.

"Go ahead, God, take my Joseph. Take my Simeon. Take my Benjamin, You can have him. In fact, take my entire household. Take my children, take my grandchildren, take my possessions, take everything from me. You can have it all. Because You are my God. I will love You and serve You to the day I die. I made a covenant with You thirty-five years ago in Shechem, and I stand by that altar. You are my God, unto death."

It's remarkable to note that in the midst of his greatest darkness and suffocating distress, Jacob never turned away from his God. He held to the vow.

SUDDEN TURN OF FORTUNE

Here is the biblical account of when Jacob finally released his sons to take Benjamin and return to Egypt for food.

> *And their father Israel said to them, "If it must be so, then do this: Take some of the best fruits of the land in your vessels and carry down a present for the man—a little balm and a little honey, spices and myrrh, pistachio nuts and almonds. Take double money in your hand, and take back in your hand the money that was returned in the mouth of your sacks; perhaps it was an oversight. Take your brother also, and arise, go back to the man. And may God Almighty give you mercy before the man, that he may release your other brother and Benjamin. If I am bereaved, I am bereaved!" (Gen. 43:11-14).*

Jacob didn't have a clue about how it was going to turn out. He had no idea that in about three to four weeks' time, everything was going to change abruptly. He couldn't see it coming.

Less than a month later, Jacob lifted his eyes and saw an Egyptian caravan headed his way. "What is an Egyptian caravan doing, coming past my house? Egyptian camels…Egyptian carts… why are the Egyptians coming past my house?"

"Wait. They're not coming *past* my house, they're coming *to* my house! What's an Egyptian caravan doing, coming to my house?"

As Jacob peered into the distance to try to make out who these Egyptians were, he paused. "That person looks familiar. Do I know him?"

It was Simeon. "Papa, it's me! Simeon! I'm b-a-a-ack!"

Then Jacob looked at another figure. "He looks familiar, too."

It was Benjamin. "Papa, it's me! Benjamin! I'm b-a-a-ack!"

Everyone could see the profound relief in Jacob's face. His two sons had returned to him.

As all the brothers drew near to their father, Judah stepped forward. "Papa, sit down. We've got to talk." Jacob was about to learn that his ten sons had been living a lie with him for twenty-two years.

"Papa," Judah was choking on his words, "I don't know how else to do this, except to just come out and say it. *Joseph is alive.*"

Jacob's jaw dropped and his eyes got wide. Trembling, he began to look around the circle of his sons, searching their faces, trying to read their intent. "Why are you doing this to me? Don't play with me on this one."

"Papa, we're not playing with you. We're telling you the truth. *Joseph is alive!*"

I am putting some of my imagination into the story. Here is the biblical account of the exchange.

> And they told him, saying, "Joseph is still alive, and he is governor over all the land of Egypt." And Jacob's heart stood still, because he did not believe them (Gen. 45:26).

Jacob could not believe they were telling him the truth. It was too good to be true.

When you've been grieving your son's death for *twenty-two years*, and then someone comes to you and says, "Your son is alive," it's too much to process. After such depth of grief, this kind of news shocks your system.

Jacob's heart stood still. He was completely stunned. He went from total blackness to blazing stadium lights in a flash. The brightness of the revelation blinded him. Stunned him. It stopped his heart.

This is characteristic of God's works. He loves to ambush His children with the greatness of His salvation.

I can almost imagine God rubbing His hands as He was planning it. "Oh, Jacob, this is going to be good. I am going to enjoy every moment of this one. Buckle up, My friend, I am about to level you with My kindness."

If you are the kind of person who likes advance notice, it may not go so well for you. Because God is into surprises. You were blindsided by adversity, but now you'll be blindsided by the glory of His mighty deliverance.

I can imagine God getting out His gun, looking at it, and thinking out loud, "Let's not kill him. Just put it on stun." When God hit Jacob with His bullet, it smashed into his chest, threw him back in his chair, and struck him so hard that it stopped his heart.

God saved it all up to hit him with it all at once.

Heart-stopping salvation.

Here it came, all at once: He had his Joseph back; he had his Simeon back; he had his Benjamin back; he got a limo ride to Egypt (an Egyptian cart); his family was established in abundant provision in Goshen; he would bless Pharaoh; he would receive the funeral of the millennium. The realization of it all came down upon his head in a moment of time.

God is so dramatic! As we've said, He's the King of drama. He loves to build the suspense so the resolution is all the more spectacular. God seemed to be silent to Jacob for many years, but it wasn't because He was withholding from him; He was intensifying the drama so that the finale would be as sensational as possible.

When Jacob spoke with Pharaoh, he described his years as "evil" (Gen. 47:9). And it was true. Up to age 130, Jacob's life was characterized largely by trials and affliction. But in the last seventeen years of his life (he died at 147), he enjoyed unparalleled blessing and prosperity. This is why Psalm 73:1 says, "Truly God is good to Israel." While the journey was unfolding, life was "evil" and difficult, but the final chapter of the story revealed that God was good to His favored son, Israel.

The occurrence of evil circumstances in our lives does not negate the goodness of God. His goodness sometimes allows evil in our lives so that His salvation ultimately might appear all the more glorious. Everything is for the fame of His name.

The Ride to Egypt

I wonder what kind of conversation Jacob had with his God as he was riding in the limo down to Egypt. I think it could have sounded something like this.

"God, everything seemed to be against me. Egypt was against me. The weather was against me. I thought that even *You* were against me. But now I see it! When You took Joseph from me—You were *for* me. When You took Simeon from me—You were *for* me. When You took Benjamin from me—You were *for* me. When You sent the famine—You were *for* me. You have been for me all along!

"Lord, You and I made a covenant thirty-five years ago in Shechem. I vowed that You would be my God. And through all the darkness and difficulty, I have held to that vow. I have served You and have never relented from that covenant, even during times when it seemed like You had forgotten our covenant. I thought I was the one holding up the covenant. But now I see it! *I'm* not the one who has kept the covenant; *You're* the one who has held up the covenant! You have been faithful to me all along. You are good. You are holy. You are merciful. You are gracious. You are kind. I worship You with all my heart. You are my God!"

Psalm 146:5 says, "Happy is he who has the God of Jacob for his help, whose hope is in the LORD his God." Happy is the man who has the God of Jacob for his help—the God who will take your hip out in order to infuse meekness into your spirit, that you might raise up a Joseph generation. Happy is the woman who has the God of Jacob for her help—the God who will take from you the darling of your eyes. Happy is the woman who has the God of Jacob for her help—the God who will take you through years of darkness and perplexity. Happy is the man who has the God of Jacob for his help—the God who will get His gun out and hit you so hard with His bullet that it will blind you, stun you, and stop your heart.

Heart-stopping salvation.

Jacob's Staff

Hebrews 11 details the manner in which many of our spiritual fathers and mothers demonstrated their faith in God. When the writer came to Jacob to show how he expressed his faith, this is what he said about him.

"By faith Jacob, when he was dying, blessed each of the sons of Joseph, and worshiped, leaning on the top of his staff" (Heb. 11:21).

I have heard it said that shepherds in olden times would en-grave a small symbol into their staff each time they had an event of unusual significance in their lives. Over the years, their staff would accrue a series of carvings which represented the most significant highlights of their journey on earth.

If this was in fact their practice, I can imagine a shepherd like Jacob sitting down with his grandchildren, pulling out his staff, and panning over the timeline of his life.

"Papa, what does this mark mean?"

"Oh, that was the time I pretended to be my brother. It's quite the story, really."

"Well Papa, what about this mark. What does this one represent?"

"That's the time I married two sisters.""And this one, Papa? What does this mark represent?"

"Sit down here, Ephraim, and let me tell you. It's a very interesting story."

Jacob's staff represented the chronicle of his entire journey. So when he leaned on that staff and worshiped, he was worshiping the God who had written the story of his life in such an amazing and complete way.

"You are good. You are generous. You are compassionate. You show Your salvation to those who love You. I went through a long, dark valley, but You brought me through and crowned me with Your mighty deliverance. Now my entire story is a living testimony—a living epistle—that testifies to Your faithfulness and grace. I love You. I delight in You. What an honor it is to stand here, at the end of my days, and worship You with my entire being. You are my God!"

This fantastic story steels my resolve to serve the God of Jacob. He'll finish my story, too.

My Baseball Story
CHAPTER 19

I've really enjoyed sharing Jacob's story with you. It displays so graphically how Jesus, history's best-selling author, uses suspense, mystery, adventure, and romance to write amazing stories with our lives.

In this final chapter, I'd like to share a story from my own life. It's one of the vignettes in my storyline that I treasure because of the promise it carries.

To tell this story, I have to go back to the summer of 1994. Sometimes I call it the summer from hell. It was in 1992 that I suffered the vocal injury to which I alluded in chapter five. Two years later, I was still fighting to continue to function as the pastor of a local church. I was no longer physically capable, however, of producing the number of words required in a week to maintain the helm of a vibrant church. My pain levels were increasing, my strength levels were decreasing, and I could read the writing on the wall: It's over.

For most pastors, when they finish at one church they move on to another. But it wasn't like that for me. What I was facing was a permanent removal from pastoral ministry. The prospect stood before me as an unbearable loss.

After all, it was God who had called me into ministry. It's all I had ever trained for. It's all I had ever lived for. Now it was being stripped away from me, and I had no idea what could possibly replace it. What does an ex-pastor with no voice do with his life?

To say I was in crisis seems like an understatement. I was in crisis professionally, physically, relationally, emotionally, and theologically. Professionally, my ministry appeared to be over; physically, my voice was reduced to a painful whisper; relationally, I could not maintain my friendships and the team I was leading; emotionally, I was under a slab of depression; theologically, I didn't understand how it was possible to be devoted to obeying Christ and take this kind of a hit. When I looked into the future, all I could see was interminable pain.

Believing that God had not revoked His ministry calling from my life (Rom. 11:29), I did my utmost to remain at my post. Pastoring a local church is a people-intensive function, however, and I was physically incapable of satisfying the social interaction the position needed. The staff and leaders of our church were incredibly compassionate for my predicament, but the fact remained that the church needed leadership.

I was giving out as many words as I could muster in a day, which meant that I was ending each day with intense pain levels. The vocal soreness, combined with the emotional and theological distress, made pastoring a very painful prospect. I even begged the Lord, "Let me resign!", but He would not release me.

I was also in great emotional distress over my inability to interact vocally with my family. Often I would come home from work with my voice completely shot and no words left for my family—I had used them all up at the office. Prior to the injury, it was my custom to lead my children enthusiastically each morning in Bible memorization and each evening in family devotions. When my voice took the hit, all of that suddenly had to stop. The inability to teach and interact with my children in itself was almost unbearable.

WORD IMMERSION

As already stated, the injury happened in 1992. For a year, I pursued medical treatment. Nobody that I consulted seemed to know what went wrong during the throat surgery. They couldn't explain why I had pain and why my vocal strength was declining. I wondered if they were too afraid of a possible lawsuit to tell me the truth. The entire ordeal was shrouded in mystery. I didn't know what caused the initial ulcer near by vocal cords; I didn't know what went wrong in the surgery; and I couldn't learn from anyone a way to recover.

The amount of mystery surrounding the whole thing became so uncanny that after a year of pursuing medical treatment, I said to my wife, "I think this is a Joseph prison. God got Joseph in prison, and God got Joseph out. If you're okay with it, Honey, I would like to make God my only consulting Physician regarding this malady."

She was agreeable with that decision, so in 1993 I began a pursuit of God in earnest. The only book I knew to go to was the Bible. All other reading was set aside, and I began to immerse myself in the Scriptures with a desperation such as I had never had.

In those days, the only thing that would break through the depression was a *rhema* word from God.[1] By *rhema* I mean a living word from the mouth of God that speaks to the situation at hand. This is why I devoted myself to word immersion. I discovered that the more time you spend in the *logos* word of God, the better your chances of receiving a *rhema*. As Jesus said, "Man shall not live by bread alone, but by every word [*rhema*] that proceeds from the mouth of God" (Mt. 4:4). It's while you're meditating in the *logos* that Jesus will sometimes speak a *rhema* to your heart. When you receive a *rhema*, now you can truly live.

Every day was an impassioned pursuit of a *rhema* word from God. I didn't receive one every day, not by any means, but whenever a *rhema* did come, it would pierce the darkness of the oppression over my mind, and I would be able to breathe for another day.

His word produces faith in the heart and hope in the spirit. Every page is encouraging and life-giving. The Bible is an amazing book—I love it!

THE SUMMER OF 1994

As the spring of 1994 approached, I grew increasingly desperate regarding my vocal situation. It was almost two years since the initial injury, and my condition had progressively deteriorated. I was still pastoring our church, but I was doing the math and knew that unless something changed I would eventually have to resign the pastorate.

---

1   There are two Greek words in the original text of the New Testament that are translated by the English, "word." They are the Greek words *logos* and *rhema*. *Logos* is often referred to as the written word of God, while *rhema* is often a reference to the spoken word of God.

As I said earlier, the Lord would not allow me to resign. At the same time, I felt like I could not continue. What do you do when you can't quit and can't continue?

In response, the elders of the church graciously offered me a six-month sabbatical. Although the church would cover my salary, I would be relieved of all responsibilities for six months so I could seek the Lord. During the summer of 1994, therefore, I was on a paid sabbatical.

"Wow!" you may be thinking, "How awesome is that? Six months on full salary, with nothing to do but enjoy the summer." In actuality, it was horrible. I was flailing like a drowning man, gasping for air, and wondering how much longer I could possibly survive. I had six months to get hold of God and figure out what was happening with my life. I felt like a man on death row.

The oppression over my soul during that summer was so thick it seemed I could cut it with a knife. If I received an insight from the word of God, it felt like a gulp of air to a drowning man. It kept me alive for a few more moments, but death seemed imminent.

The worst part of my week was going to church. I felt it was the right thing before God to take my family to church each weekend during the sabbatical, even though I had no responsibilities in the services. Dragging myself to church was intensely difficult because of the shame and reproach I felt. Our church had three weekend services at the time, so I would go to the Saturday night service to get it over with.

Black Sabbath

I remember this one weekend as being particularly dark. It was Saturday, which meant going to church, and I was dreading it. A cloud of oppression lay thick upon my mind and I was doing my utmost to shake it. I spent several hours that day in prayer and the word, but I couldn't escape the looming dread of the Saturday evening service.

The thing that comforted me was the thought, "Okay, I'll go to church tonight; but then I'll get up tomorrow, get in my reading chair, and meditate in the word. Perhaps God will speak something to my heart tomorrow. If He does, I know the clouds will break, a shaft of sunlight will penetrate my soul, and I'll be able to live for one more day."

So we went to the Saturday service. After coming home, I went straight to bed. Then I got up Sunday morning, settled into my chair with my Bible, and began to implore God for a *rhema*. "Please! Please! Please!"

Nothing.

I tried praying.

Dust bowl.

That went on for two or three hours.

Finally, I literally threw my Bible on the ground and declared in my soul, "That's it! I've had it! Enough! Me, me, me. My, my, my. Navel-gazing, introspective, self-centered, fetal-position, pity party, my myopic world of pain. Yuck, I hate this! All this preoccupation with myself is nauseating. If I'm going to hurt this much, my kids are going to have fun today. I'm taking them to a baseball game!"

Now, I was raised in a good Christian home, and in our tradition Christians didn't go to baseball games on Sunday. Sunday was the Lord's Day (Rev. 1:10); it was a day for worship and rest, not for sports activities. In fact, in our tradition, Christians rarely went to baseball games, period. So I had never been to one of these games. And I had certainly never been to a sports event on a Sunday! But I was in too much pain to care about the rules.

I threw my three kids—Joel, Katie, and Michael—into our minivan, grabbed a couple neighborhood boys, and off we went to Silver Stadium in Rochester, New York. My wife didn't want to go, so it was just me and the five kids.

Rochester has a triple-A ball team called the Red Wings. They happened to be playing a home game that afternoon. As I said, it was my first time to one of their games, but I was trying to play it cool with the kids. I was pretending to know my way around, but inside I felt like a first-timer in church. "Where do you park?" "How do you get in?" "How much is it?" "Where are our seats?" "Where are the bathrooms?"

Finally we found our way to the bleachers. Katie sat next me. After her were the four boys in a row. I was in an ornery mood: "Everybody gets popcorn. Everyone gets a Coke. Everybody gets a hotdog." My kids were sitting there, stuffing their faces, their caps on, gloves in hand. It was seventy-five degrees, not a cloud in the sky, a mid-August Sunday afternoon in Upstate New York.

Baseball in America. Picture perfect.

It was a gorgeous afternoon, but the cloud of oppression over my mind had not budged an inch. I was glad my kids were having fun, but I was absolutely miserable.

WHICH VOICE TO BELIEVE?

I began to talk to myself. "I wonder if God knows where I'm at." I didn't mean, "I wonder if God knows that I'm at a baseball game on a Sunday afternoon." What I meant was, "I wonder if God knows how I'm feeling right now. I'm spending all my time in the word and prayer—I mean, they're *paying* me to pray right now. And even though I'm coming after God as hard as I know to, I can't shake the oppression over my mind. I have no idea what else to do. Am I losing my mind? This thing called Christianity is not working for me right now. God, do You even understand where I'm at?"

Then my self-talk took another turn. "What have I done? Why are You so angry with me? I must have done something terribly wrong to get You this angry. You're taking *everything* away from me. If You would just tell me what I've done, I would gladly repent, and we could put all this behind us. Talk to me. What have I done?"

When you're in an emotionally tender place like that, I swear you have a demon parked on your shoulder, because I had this megaphone voice blaring in my ear, "Rejected! Abandoned! Forsaken! It's over! You're under the wrath of God. Every war has casualties. You're just a casualty in the war. You're a has-been. Get in reality. It's over!" All the natural data in my body confirmed that that was the voice of truth.

But did I hear another voice in the other ear? No, surely not. This blaring voice, this is the voice of reason. But did I hear another whispering voice? Could it possibly be the still, small voice of the Holy Spirit? *"I am with you. I have chosen you. I am for you. I'm closer than ever. This thing is going somewhere. I'm writing a story with your life. It's not over."*

I desperately wanted to believe that I was hearing God's small voice—that He likes me, He's for me, that He has a divine purpose for my life, that His affections are upon me. O how I wanted all that to be true! But the loud voice was so overwhelming, and it seemed to be corroborated by all the data at the natural level. How could I know that I was actually hearing the Lord's still, small voice in the midst of all the cacophony?

As I sat in the stadium stands, wrestling between the two voices, this crazy idea floated through my brain. Ask God for a sign.

"No! I will not ask God if I can catch a baseball as a sign that I
am, in fact, hearing His voice. I am not asking God for a sign that
He loves me, that He's for me." My parents had trained me well.
They had taught me that you don't tempt the Lord God by asking
Him for signs in that manner.

"I am not asking God to let me catch a baseball as a sign that
He is for me. Stop this crazy thinking!"

I tried to shut the stupid idea out of my mind, but I couldn't.
Then the thought sort of morphed into this: "I wonder if He would
let me catch a baseball. I'm not asking for one. But would He *let* me
catch a baseball, as a sign that He loves me and is writing a story
with my life?"

Again, I tried to shut down this treacherous line of thinking.
"Stop it, Bob! This is a bad way to think. If you think you're depressed now, just wait, you're about to get *really* depressed."

But I could not get the crazy thought out of my head.

My analytical side kicked in and I started calculating my
chances. I mean, I had never been to one of these games before, so
what were my chances of catching a baseball?

DOING THE MATH, πR^2

Instinctively, my mind began calculating the odds. I was looking at the radius of the ball field. I was estimating how many fans
were in the stands. I was counting how many balls were being
caught by fans. "They're not catching baseballs."

Besides that, we were in a section of bleachers that was protected by an overhang—there was another level of bleachers over
our heads—so a ball wouldn't be able to reach our section of seats
even if it wanted to. "*Stop it!*" I had done the math. There's no way.

I did my best to push the crazy notion from my mind.

POP FLY

We were about three quarters of the way through the game
by now. One of the Rochester Red Wings was up to bat. He hit a
fly ball that was going foul. As it approached the stands, with one
motion hundreds of fans rose simultaneously to their feet. Gloves

appeared out of nowhere. I had never seen so many baseball gloves in one location at one time. Hands reached to the heavens. And I was on my feet with the rest of the fools.

As the ball approached our section, it was clear that it was not coming in our direction. It was off to my left. It came underneath the overhang, but then hit one of the crossbeams that supported the flooring over our heads, careened off the crossbeam at a *bizarre* angle, and came flying down straight at me. It came at me so fast that I didn't know what to do with it. It pushed through my hands, past my arms, bounced off my chest, and landed squarely in my daughter, Katie's, lap.

I sank into my seat next to her, stunned. "Daddy, I got a baseball!" she squealed with delight. I couldn't talk to her, but inside I was thinking, "That's not *your* baseball, Sweetheart, that's *my* baseball!"

I handled the ball and just stared at it. It was real. I was holding it. God had given me a baseball.

An elderly gentleman sitting in front of me turned and said, "I've been coming to this stadium every week for over thirty years, and I've never caught a baseball."

I don't know if my interpretation is correct, but here's what I took the ball to mean. "I am with you. I am for you. I love you. I understand where you're at. I love the way you're pursuing Me. Don't quit now. I'm writing a story with your life. Let Me finish what I've started. You have a hope and a future."

One of my kids ended up with the ball in their hands, and I especially like that part of the story. Because my journey, and everything represented by that baseball, has everything to do with the destiny of my children—and their children.

I call that baseball my "kiss from heaven." It was a sign from God, in the face of my greatest darkness, of His affection and good intentions for my life.

This story continues to energize my resolve—I refuse to abort the story. By His grace, I am going to continue to abide in the love of Christ and be strengthened in faith. This isn't my last chapter.

Nor have you seen your last chapter, either. Persevere in the grace of God and let Jesus finish what He's writing. May you come through this trial "perfect, and complete, lacking nothing."

Amen!

Lessons from Jacob's Life

Jacob's life reveals some valuable insights that I didn't share earlier because I didn't want to break up the cadence of the story. I hope these insights, collected here somewhat randomly, are as helpful to you as they've been to me.

Waiting on God

Jacob was the only person in Genesis to talk about waiting on God. While prophesying over his sons, he stopped to exclaim, "I have waited for your salvation, O LORD!" (Gen. 49:18). The statement appears out of place in its context, but when you realize how waiting was so central to Jacob's story, it makes sense. Even though it took many years, eventually he saw the day when God sent from heaven and saved him.

After Jacob, the Scriptures are virtually silent on the discipline of waiting on God until the advent of David. The whole thing burst to life in David's writings. David's psalmist anointing, which was fueled from a place of long and loving meditation in the word, necessitated an awakening to waiting on God in His presence. Perhaps it is not accidental that as the first scriptural writer to place considerable focus on the grace of waiting, David was also very taken with Jacob. David mentions Jacob in his writings more than any other patriarch.

After David, the next Bible author to pick up the banner of waiting on God was Isaiah. Isaiah is "the king of wait." Is it accidental that he mentions the name of Jacob forty-two times? Both David and Isaiah placed profound significance upon Jacob as an example for us to follow.

"Waiting" is an excellent word to summarize Jacob's life. It's true that over his span of 147 years he had some bell-ringing, catalytic moments. But the vast majority of his story was marked by extended periods of waiting on God. Brief bursts of divine activity were separated by vast expanses of virtual inactivity.

Actually, this is one of God's signature ways. He separates His most outstanding works by protracted periods of seeming silence. Then, when He finally manifests His glory, it shines all the more brilliantly. Consider the lengthy span between each of God's most outstanding wonders: from creation to the flood, to the exodus, to the return from exile, to the resurrection of Christ, and then to the future coming of Christ. There's a long time between each of those six mighty events! It's those prolonged lapses between His major activities that put the flair into the way God invades and redirects human history. The deafening silence of the thousands of years between each mighty intervention has rumbled throughout history in timpanic drumrolls of suspenseful anticipation.

The waiting seasons actually give God the room He needs to write the story. Those who demand resolution too hastily can forfeit the grandeur of what God was intending to write. By taking things into your own hands prematurely, you can undermine the basis upon which God was planning to write your last, great chapter.

> *For since the beginning of the world men have not heard nor perceived by the ear, nor has the eye seen any God besides You, who acts for the one who waits for Him (Isa. 64:4).*

Takeaway: Wait on God. Give Him some material to work with.

WRESTLING TO BE A PRINCE

In the wrestling match with Christ, Jacob asked Him to tell His name.

> *And He said, "Your name shall no longer be called Jacob, but Israel; for you have struggled with God and with men, and have prevailed." Then Jacob asked, saying, "Tell me Your name, I pray." And He said, "Why is it that you ask about My name?" (Gen. 32:28-29).*

Jesus did not divulge His name to Jacob. But if He had, He might have said to him, "Israel." Because Israel is one of the names of Christ. This is seen in Isaiah.

And He said to me, "You are My servant, O Israel, in whom I will be glorified" (Isa. 49:3).

This verse appears in the "Servant songs" of Isaiah. The context clearly indicates that the Father is the speaker, and He is talking to His Son, the Servant. The Father, addressing His Son, calls Him Israel.

Israel means "Prince with God." Truly Jesus is the ultimate Prince with God! He wears the name gloriously. Jesus is the true Israel of God. To be in Israel, you must be in Christ, because Christ is Israel.

At Peniel, Jacob was wrestling with Israel! When Jesus gave Jacob the name Israel, He was giving him His own name.

Jacob did not really understand it at the time, but he was wrestling for his name. "If you are to be a Prince with God, Jacob, you are going to have to wrestle down the name."

Takeaway: To wear the name Christ has for you, don't be surprised if you have to wrestle it down.

ABRAHAM, ISAAC, AND JACOB

Several times in Scripture, God identified Himself as the God of Abraham, the God of Isaac, and the God of Jacob (e.g. Ex. 3:6). Let me explain one reason why that designation is significant to me personally. It helps me define who I serve.

In today's world of multiple gods, I consider it wise to identify precisely which God I serve. I serve the God of Abraham. But I need to be more specific because Abraham had several sons (1 Chron. 1:32). I do not serve the God of Ishmael (one of Abraham's sons), but the God of Isaac.

But even that is not precise enough because Isaac had two sons, Esau and Jacob. I do not serve the God of Esau but of Jacob.

Still, that is not specific enough in today's world because two major world religions (Judaism and Christianity) trace their roots to Jacob. I serve the God who gave to Jacob the name Israel. In other words, I serve the God and Father of Jesus Christ.

Yes, I can tell you exactly which God I serve. My God is the God of Abraham, the God of Isaac, the God of Jacob, and the God of Jesus of Nazareth (Acts 3:13). For me, there is no other.

Takeaway: Serve the only and true God of Jacob: the God and Father of our Lord Jesus Christ.

THE HARD WAY

We learn from Jacob's life that sometimes God wants things to transpire the hard way. God could have made everything so much easier on Jacob by just saying to him, "Jacob, go down to Egypt." God led Abraham down to Egypt, and He could have just as easily done the same with Jacob.

But instead, God put the squeeze on Jacob. First, he lost Joseph; then he lost Simeon; and the man in Egypt was wanting Benjamin next. Add to that, the intense distress from the famine. His entire household was hungry! The combination of stress factors put incredible pressure on God's beloved servant. He went through all kinds of emotional gyrations before he was finally presented with the solution of going to Egypt to meet Joseph.

After Jacob was finally settled in Egypt, I can imagine him wondering, "Lord, why did You make it so hard on me? I would have happily followed Your voice. All You had to do was say to me, 'Move to Egypt.' Why did You make it come down the hard way?"

The truth is that often God leads His favorites in the hard way. (The leading example, of course, is the cross of Christ.) Why? Because God accomplishes so many things at multiple levels by letting the thing happen the hard way. He uses the difficulty to excavate hearts and produce greater eternal fruit than if an easier path had been taken.

Takeaway: Do not be thrown off balance if God allows a portion of your journey to come down the hard way.

EVEN NUMBERS

I have noticed that sometimes God uses even numbers, or numbers with a meaningful association, to draw attention to the significance of a certain person's story in that moment. Let me give a few examples.

Enoch walked with God for 365 years, and then God took him (Gen. 5:24). Why did God not take him at age 364 or at 366? God waited until Enoch was precisely 365 because of the significance of the number. That number in itself was a message from God: "I want to walk with man 365 days a year in unbroken fellowship."

God waited to send the flood until Noah was precisely six hundred years old (Gen. 7:6). Why the even number? To indicate that God's timing was based not on some calendar in heaven but on the calendar of Noah's life. Through his faith and righteousness, Noah became a timepiece and chronometer to his generation of heaven's movements in the earth. This underscored the significance of Noah as the man at that time around whom God was writing human history.

How old was Abraham when Isaac was born? One hundred. The even number arrests us. It tells us, "Look at Abraham. He's My man. What I am doing with him right now is very important."

Moses' life divides into three forty-year periods. The timing of the exodus and entrance into the promised land was calibrated to the life of one man, Moses. 40, 80, 120 years. The emphasis of those even numbers highlighted the importance of Moses in God's redemptive plan.

God waited to lead Israel out of Egypt until their exodus fell precisely on 430 years to the day since God had spoken to Abraham (Ex. 12:41). This was God's way of saying, "This is purposeful. Pay attention."

Several men are emphasized in the Bible by making significant moments happen when they were thirty years old. At age thirty, Joseph rose from the prison to the palace; David became king of Judah; God visited Ezekiel (Ezek. 1:1); John the Baptist's ministry was launched; Christ Jesus' ministry was launched. Quite often God lines up everything on earth to the timeline of His servant, so that he literally becomes God's calendar.

Now, here's how this principle applies to Jacob. The Bible makes a point of noting that when God brought His salvation to Jacob's life and brought him down to Egypt, Jacob was 130 (Gen. 47:9). The even number is intended to alert us. God did not deliver him at 131, but at an even 130.

At this juncture in Jacob's narrative, Joseph was 39. Some readers might think that Joseph was the key character in the story at this point, but the use of the numbers tells us otherwise. If Joseph were the main player, God would have waited one year until

Joseph was 40 and Jacob 131. But no, Joseph was to be 39, and Jacob was to be an even 130. The numbers, just by themselves, tell us who the primary person is at that moment. Jacob is the man. It is his story that we are to behold.

Takeaway: Be watchful for ways in which God uses numbers to bring emphasis to your story.

Compounded Generational Blessings

Jacob was desperate to receive the blessing of his father, Isaac. The intensity of Jacob's desire for the blessing pointed to its significance. The blessing that Isaac had to give was powerful and eternally important. But now here's a stunning statement from Jacob, as he spoke to his sons.

The blessings of your father have excelled the blessings of my ancestors,
up to the utmost bound of the everlasting hills (Gen. 49:26).

Jacob was telling his sons, "As much as I wanted my father's blessing, I have more to give than he. What I have to give greatly excels the blessing of my father, as high as the everlasting hills."[1] The implication of his statement is, "I wanted my father's blessing desperately and did my utmost to get it. How you have lived your lives has demonstrated how badly each of you, in turn, have wanted the blessing that I have to give."

Reuben, the firstborn, obviously did not earnestly covet his father's blessing. You don't sleep with your father's wife if you are passionate about receiving his blessing.

Of the twelve sons, Joseph was the one who demonstrated the greatest zeal to receive his father's blessing, so he was the one who got the greatest share.

Genesis 49:26 (above) shows that Jacob had become a profoundly spiritual man. The deposit of grace that he was able to pass to his sons was richer and deeper than the grace on Abraham or Isaac.

Takeaway: You have more to give your children than your parents gave you. Your pinnacle becomes your children's platform.

---

1   Isaiah 58:13-14 also speaks of the heritage Jacob has for his believing children, which enables them "to ride on the high hills of the earth."

A GRANDFATHER ANOINTING

When Joseph brought his two sons to Jacob for a blessing, Jacob crossed his arms, placing his right hand on the younger grandson.

> *Now when Joseph saw that his father laid his right hand on the head of Ephraim, it displeased him; so he took hold of his father's hand to remove it from Ephraim's head to Manasseh's head. And Joseph said to his father, "Not so, my father, for this one is the firstborn; put your right hand on his head." But his father refused and said, "I know, my son, I know. He also shall become a people, and he also shall be great; but truly his younger brother shall be greater than he, and his descendants shall become a multitude of nations." So he blessed them that day, saying, "By you Israel will bless, saying, 'May God make you as Ephraim and as Manasseh!'" And thus he set Ephraim before Manasseh (Gen. 48:17-20).*

Joseph was thinking analytically. He thought it proper for his father to place his right hand upon the firstborn. Jacob, however, was functioning out of his spirit, not his head. In the Spirit, Jacob perceived a greater inheritance for the younger Ephraim.

The grandfather had greater clarity into the calling and destiny of the sons than the father. Where Joseph was clouded, Jacob could see.

It was not uncommon in Scripture for fathers to lack discernment regarding their sons. For example, Isaac favored Esau, even though Jacob was God's choice. Jesse favored his oldest sons, although David was God's choice. Joseph favored Manasseh when Ephraim was God's choice. Preconceived ideas can blind a father from accurately recognizing the grace and anointing that rests upon a certain child. This is where the perceptivity of a godly grandfather can complete the picture.

Takeaway for grandparents: Ask God for an anointing in the Holy Spirit to call forth the destiny of your grandchildren.

INTIMACY MAKES IT PERSONAL

At the end of his life, Jacob made a statement that is easy to gloss over and not fully absorb. Jacob uttered these words in the context of his blessing over his son, Joseph.

> *But his bow remained in strength, and the arms of his hands were made strong by the hands of the Mighty God of Jacob (from there is the Shepherd, the Stone of Israel) (Gen.* 49:24*).*

In this verse, Jacob described God as "the Mighty God of Jacob." It was quite a bold affirmation. It was a very assertive way to say, "He is my God."

If I were to use the same language, I would say, "He is the Mighty God of Bob." Go ahead, insert in your own name there. Do you have the confidence—the ownership—to call Him the God of (insert your name)?

I wonder what kind of intimacy and conviction rested in the bosom of Jacob when he spoke to his children of "the Mighty God of Jacob." The confidence behind this assertion came as a result of God's salvation in his life. God showed His salvation by returning Joseph, Simeon, and Benjamin to him, and providing abundantly for his family in Goshen. That's when Jacob realized how vested God was personally in their relationship.

When God took Jacob's hip out, Jacob took it personally; then, when God restored Jacob's losses, Jacob realized that the whole story was profoundly personal to God, too. The affection between them was torrential. It was all about love and loyalty.

I am asking God to finish my story in such a manner that at the end of my race I might be able to talk to my children, like Jacob, about "the God of Bob."

Takeaway: By the time your last chapter is complete, may it be that personal for you, too.

All of Bob Sorge's Titles

EXPLORING WORSHIP:
  A Practical Guide to Praise & Worship $16
Exploring Worship WORKBOOK & DISCUSSION GUIDE .... $ 5
IN HIS FACE: A Prophetic Call to Renewed Focus $13
THE FIRE OF DELAYED ANSWERS $14
THE FIRE OF GOD'S LOVE $13
PAIN, PERPLEXITY, AND PROMOTION:
  A Prophetic Interpretation of the Book of Job $14
DEALING WITH THE REJECTION AND PRAISE OF MAN $10
GLORY: When Heaven Invades Earth $10
SECRETS OF THE SECRET PLACE $15
Secrets of the Secret Place: COMPANION STUDY GUIDE $11
Secrets of the Secret Place: LEADER'S MANUAL .... $ 5
ENVY: The Enemy Within $12
FOLLOWING THE RIVER: A Vision for Corporate Worship $10
LOYALTY: The Reach of the Noble Heart $14
UNRELENTING PRAYER $13
POWER OF THE BLOOD: Approaching God with Confidence ... $13
IT'S NOT BUSINESS, IT'S PERSONAL $10
OPENED FROM THE INSIDE: Taking the Stronghold of Zion $11
MINUTE MEDITATIONS $12
BETWEEN THE LINES: God is Writing Your Story $13

DVD Series:
EXPLORING WORSHIP DVD SERIES $30
SECRETS OF THE SECRET PLACE DVD SERIES $30

To order Bob's materials:

- Go to www.oasishouse.com
- Call 816-767-8880 (ask about our excellent quantity discounts)
- Write Oasis House, PO Box 522, Grandview, MO 64030-0522

Go to www.oasishouse.com for special package discounts, book descriptions, ebooks, and free teachings.